Motorcycle road racing in the fifties

MOTORCYCLE ROAD RACING IN THE FIFTIES

An illustrated review – 1949 to 1959

ANDREW McKINNON

Published in 1982 by Osprey Publishing Limited,
12-14 Long Acre, London WC2E 9LP
A member company of the George Philip Group

British Library Cataloguing in Publication Data
McKinnon, Andrew
   Motorcycle road racing in the fifties.
  1.   Motorcycle racing—History
  I.   Title
  796. 7′5′09045   GV1060

   ISBN 0-85045-405-5

Editor Tim Parker

Typeset by Tameside Filmsetting Limited,
Ashton-under-Lyne, Lancashire, and printed by
Butler and Tanner Ltd, Frome and London

Contents

Introduction

Motorcycle road racing in the fifties is designed to give the enthusiast an accurate, concise reference to those important formative years of the world championships as we know them today.

Here you will find the information to settle those arguments about yesteryear . . . the principal stars, the machinery, the circuits, the championships and a complete list of world championships results from 1949–1959.

This volume, with its 150 illustrations paints the picture of how road racing used to be 30 years ago, right from the chivalrous Freddie Frith and his clean sweep of the very first 300 cc world championship to a youngster called Mike Hailwood recording the first of an avalanche of grand prix victories at the end of the decade.

The reader will have to bear in mind that this book deals with a specific period and therefore some of the chapters or passages may seem a little unjust towards a certain personality or machine. To explain this point the publishers, excited by the growing interest in nostaglia in the motorcycle field, are planning a further two volumes covering the ensuing two decades and any short-comings in this first edition will certainly be remedied in the future.

By the end of the intensive period of research the final product should be a comprehensive account of the history of the sport to the present day with a complete check on world championship results the men who achieved them and the machinery on which they carried out their tasks.

For those who can remember those days of 'true grit' on the race track it should bring the memories flooding back and for those who have been weaned on the more sophisticated machinery of today it should present an eye-opening contrast between the years.

Many of the illustrations you will find in this record of 10 years history have never been published before. It would have been easy simply to have gone to the archives of the trade press and reproduced photographs which have been seen time and again. But that was not the aim of our project.

We wanted to bring knowledge, scattered over a whole range of previous accounts and still in enthusiast's heads, within the same cover and intersperse it with the very best that photographic sources could provide.

Hopefully we achieved our aim but it wasn't an easy task with one newspaper's archives dating back only 25 years!

To record every single fact to emerge from a decade's racing is a virtually impossible task, thousands of significant happenings, great and small, take place. Contained in the following pages are, hopefully, the more important milestones of the 1950s at least in our opinion.

It should provide a clear picture of how times changed visually and statistically and hopefully provide hours of entertainment as you relive one of the most colourful periods of our road racing heritage.

Whatever your age it should provide a useful addition to your reference library . . . a way of turning back the clock at the flick of a page.

1

The machines– The Grand Prix contenders

AJS Benelli BMW BSA DKW Ducati Gilera
Guzzi Matchless Mondial Morini MV Agusta MZ
NSU Norton Triumph Velocette Vincent

AJS

Of all the marques in the history of world championship road racing the name of AJS must rank among the best known of all.

The factory became universally known for its 7R 'boy racer' and between 1948 and 1962 475 of these economy racers were produced.

Introduced in late 1948 the 350 cc 7R was destined to become one of the greatest pieces of raceware with a popularity comparible to that of today's Yamaha racers, predominant in world championship and international events.

In 1949, the first year of the FIM governed world series, the 350 machine from AJS's stable lived under the shadow of the 500 cc twin cylinder Porcupine, a legendary model from the Plumstead factory but one whose existence was far shorter than that of its smaller capacity sister.

The late Les Graham on the 500 cc AJS Porcupine. He won the factory their only world title in 1949

The late Les Graham won AJS their only world title during the very first world championship season. His success came on a Porcupine with wins at the Ulster Grand Prix, at the Swiss Grand Prix and a second place at the Dutch TT. World championship races numbered less than half those of today's more demanding series.

That year Graham was well backed up by team mate Bill Doran. He won the Belgian Grand Prix, was fourth at the Ulster and third at Monza. His efforts, combined with Graham's, earned AJS the world manufacturers title that season.

But on the Isle of Man TT front things were not so bright for the British factory and of course, as remains the story today, success on the longest circuit in the world is of paramount importance.

In fact their real breakthrough wasn't to come until 1954 when New Zealander Rod Coleman won the Junior TT on a 350 cc three valve single. It was so ironic that AJS's machines which really did prove themselves in the way of results, ie. the Porcupine and the triple knocker, had a very limited life span. For like

With the Compliments of
A.J.S. MOTOR CYCLES
LONDON, S.E.18.
AND MOTOR CYCLE

R. L. Graham
1949 500 c.c. CLASS
ROAD RACING CHAMPION OF THE WORLD.

MOTOR CYCLE
Photograph.

the Porcupine, the 7R 3A which Coleman used in 1954, was soon abandoned.

AJS began the decade on a shaky note. After Graham's exciting year in 1949 the 7R began struggling against the tried and tested opposition of the sohc and dohc Velocettes and the new Norton 'featherbed' eclipsed the performance of the Porc. In fact Graham's only win during 1950 came at the rain-soaked Swiss Grand Prix. He completed a double with victory at 350 level.

After suffering indignities in 1950 AJS realised that things were not going to get any easier in the grand prix arena and that they would have to respond accordingly. Their engineers worked overtime to bring their machines into line with the more successful racing machines. They reduced the valve angle and gave the intake port a more acute angle on the 7R. The engine was mounted further forward to improve handling and the wheelbase was reduced to 55 in. The finishing touches were given with a narrower set of crankcases and the introduction of clip-ons in conjunction with the shortening of the front forks by an inch.

Similar work was carried out on the Porcupine cycle parts. After monitoring the effects of the initial improvements in 1951 AJS in 1952 raised the engine to 45 degrees and reduced its weight by re-locating the sump under the motor.

In that same year the 350 model benefitted from even more sweeping changes in the fight against the other factories. A three valve engine was introduced, the one which was to give Coleman his career best result two years later.

AJS seemed to be countering the Velocette challenge well and towards the end of 1952 the revamped machine set a new 350 cc one hour world speed record at 115.66 mph.

The three valve version of the 7R was designed by Ike Hatch but one of the most significant chapters in the development of the machine came when Jack Williams, whose son Peter was to go on to become one of the most successful racers of the early and mid-70s,

Pictured at the 1950 TT, a 500 cc twin cylinder AJS Porcupine. It was the factory's most successful machine

joined AMC, the company formed when Matchless took over the original AJS operation.

Williams was not given the benefit of working on the three valve motor which of course had more scope for development. Instead his brief on joining the company was to get as much out of the two valve engine as he could with a very strict budget, thus keeping its price down.

He worked wonders. After six years of work he boosted the power of the two valve 7R power unit from 37 bhp at 7500 rpm to 42 bhp at 7800 rpm. Many experts at the time speculated on what would have happened had Williams been allowed to breath on the triple knocker engine. It would almost certainly have extended the machine's life beyond 1962 but unfortunately the 7R 3A was phased out after its TT success.

Only a month after that triumphant TT appearance a 7R 3B model had been completed at the factory which revved to 8000 rpm but management policy prevented it from being raced.

When Williams arrived at AMC the only success which the two valve 7R engine had experienced was a win in the Junior Manx Grand Prix in 1952 in the hands of Bob McIntyre. By the time Williams had exhausted the potential of his charge the two valve engine was kicking out more power than the TT winner!

But 1954 brought good news and bad news for the British racing enthusiast. The Junior TT victory for AJS may have added spice to the battle which raged among the UK factories but that same year AJS decided to give up any serious challenge they may have had in the 500 cc class.

The reason? The emergence of the major Italian forces which were to reign supreme in the 500 class until 1975. Success in the immediate post war years was possible for the home factories because their foreign opponents had committed themselves to supercharging.

The FIM destroyed all that when they decreed that there would be no blown machines at the start of the world championships proper. By the time the 50's were two or three years old the irate overseas engineers

LEFT ABOVE *New Zealander Rod Coleman with the triple knocker on which he won the 1954 Junior TT. The machine's life was a short one*

LEFT BELOW *Alan Shepherd was one of a host of British stars who chose AJS. Shepherd is pictured at Scarborough in 1958*

BELOW *Australian campaigner Harry Hinton gets the most out of his 7R at Brands Hatch in 1958*

had made up for lost time and were nibbling away at the British dominance.

By 1954 the process was complete and AJS made their decision to throw in the towel with their 500 cc grand prix programme.

The signs had all been there in the 1954 TT series. The Italian's multis had become too quick for AJS. The Porcupines struggled that year. Coleman, Farrant and McIntyre were the pilots and none of them finished high up. McIntyre was 14th when the attrocious weather stopped the race and Coleman had worked his way up to fifth after three laps only to have his fuel tank split.

But the decision to end 500 cc competition as a factory did not mean the last of the name in the class. After an absence of five years AJS returned to the race track with the G50—a direct descendant of the 7R but marketed under the Matchless banner.

The big single pumped out 47 bhp at 7200 rpm and although slower than its main competitor, the Manx Norton, its simple single-ohc engine which was easy to tune and maintain made it a very popular buy among the privateers of the day.

Initially the G50 featured 7R valves but when it officially appeared in 1959 as the successor to the G45 Matchless it had its own personal exhaust size of $1\frac{3}{4}$ in.

The G50 survived for four years and during that time 180 machines left the factory.

ABOVE *Another satisfied customer. J. W. Waller aboard his 350 cc 'boy racer' at Brands Hatch in 1959. Their popularity was unrivalled!*

BELOW *A picture of determination. Brilliant Scot Bob McIntyre and his 7R at Silverstone in May 1959*

Benelli

The Italian Benelli factory's successes were concentrated around the opening years of the decade thanks to the efforts of their brave works rider Dario Ambrosini. The Benelli brothers, who founded the company, had, like many of their counterparts planned their strategy for the post war years with supercharging in mind but the FIM's ruling ruined their development programme and after some initial success through Ted Mellors who won the 1939 Lightweight TT, ending a DKW and Moto Guzzi dominance, they had to wait until Ambrosini began displaying his brilliance on their unblown machines.

First signs of a recovery in the racing world from Benelli came in 1949 when Ambrosini finished runner-up in the 250 world championship. A year later he was world champion and his brilliant individual effort had also been enough to give his company the manufacturers title. Highspot of that triumphant year was his appearance at the Isle of Man TT races. After a slow start and with a two and a half gallon handicap over the other machines in the lightweight class, he came through to thrash the opposition which was no push over with the likes of Maurice Cann in the race on the works Moto Guzzi. At the flag Ambrosini held a six yard advantage over his nearest rival and that was after three and a half hours!

The machine Ambrosini used in those victorious days was a developed version of the pre-war dohc single. The factory had hoped to use their exciting four cylinder 250 designed with supercharging in mind but legislation rendered that bike defunct before it was even raced.

It was in 1951 that Benelli were to pull out of racing for the bulk of the 50's. Ambrosini was killed while practising for the French Grand Prix at the five and a half mile Albi circuit. He skidded on a patch of wet tar and collided with a telegraph pole.

Earlier that year Benelli had lost out on the lightweight TT by 8.4 seconds to Tommy Wood on the Moto Guzzi because of a carburation error. Benelli paid the penalty for only running one rider in the world championships. When Ambrosini was killed they could not contest the remaining grands prix and finished the year in third place in the 250 series which was won by Bruno Ruffo (Moto Guzzi).

Had it not been for the tragic accident at the French Grand Prix the Italian factory would almost certainly

Journalist Graham Walker was privileged in 1950 to give Dario Ambrosini's TT-winning 250 Benelli a test spin up the Mountain Mile

have continued racing and add more of an influence on competition during that era.

When at last Benelli did decide to return to grand prix racing in the 50's their attempt to reach their former heights was blocked by the Japanese invasion which was just beginning in the 250 class.

But they were to return yet again towards the end of the following decade.

RIGHT ABOVE *Dickie Dale (22) and Silvio Grassetti give the 250 cc Benelli single its big time debut at the 1959 Imola Gold Cup*

BELOW RIGHT *Close up of one of the Benelli power units. The factory withdrew from grand prix racing in 1951 and did not return until later in the decade*

BELOW *When Benelli returned to world championship racing in the late 1950s their machinery had an altogether more refined look about it. Their attempts to reach their former heights was thwarted*

BMW

The Bavarian Motor Works of Munich had a cruel introduction to the 50's as a result of the Nazis ravaging their works during the Second World War, and confiscating all their records and tools. Production of motor cycles could not resume again until 1947 but by 1953 more than 10,000 machines had rolled off their production lines.

But the history of the factory's 500 cc grand prix engine dates to the 1930's when Otto Ley and Karl Gall gave everybody a taste of the expertise which the factory possessed.

The power was there but sadly lacking were the handling capabilities of the solo machines. Indeed that

LEFT ABOVE *One of the most successful BMW sidecar partnerships, Walter Schneider and Hans Strauss on their 500 cc outfit at Scarborough in 1955*

LEFT BELOW *Walter Zeller, BMW's leading solo rider, whose skills were held back by the poor handling qualities of the machine*

BELOW *Three times world sidecar champion during the 1950s, Willi Noll, in action at the 1956 Isle of Man TT races*

is one of the biggest reasons that the BMW power unit became so successful in sidecar outfits. It was the engine's unique flat cylinder layout which made it perfect for sidecar use and from 1954 to 1975, apart from 1968–1971, BMW won every world title in the sidecar class.

Before the outbreak of war BMW's solo successes were creditable but when peace returned, with the banning of superchargers and Germany being on probation they struggled. With little significance in international events the factory maintained its reputation at home and in 1950 the legendary Georg Meier used a pre-War compressor model to average 129.87 mph, with a record lap of 134.21 mph at Rheyit.

The ban on supercharging forced the BMW boffins back to the drawing board and by 1953 they had come up with their unblown challenger, the 500 cc Rennsport.

In the solo classes during the 50's BMW suffered the ultimate frustration. With their leading solo rider Walter Zeller they scored plenty of second to sixth places but could not make the big breakthrough. In desperation they introduced fuel injection to their grand prix racers but still they could not compare with

the Italian factory fours. But what the factory lacked in terms of success in the solo world it more than compensated for with its phenomenal record in the threewheeler class. In fact BMW is the most prolific sidecar force in the history of the world championships.

It was the fact that Fritz Hillebrand and Wilhelm Noll finished second and third respectively behind Eric Oliver's Norton in his swansong TT in 1954 which alerted the racing world to BMW's coming. From then on they, quite simply, didn't look back. Noll went on to win the world title and it was a grip on world championship racing which they were to hold until 1968 when Helmut Fath's URS broke the stranglehold. During his heyday Noll became the fastest sidecar driver in the world when he took his faired BMW down the Ingolstadt autobahn in 1955 at 174 mph.

The factory's post war achievements in the solo field aren't really worth noting save for the fourth place in the 1956 Senior TT achieved by Walter Zeller.

ABOVE *Dickie Dale tried his luck on a BMW in the 1959 Senior TT without success. Like Walter Zeller and Geoff Duke he found his pairing with the German bike a frustrating one*

LEFT ABOVE *In the twilight of his career Geoff Duke added his name to the list of BMW owners. Here he chases an opponent at Governors Bridge during the 1958 TT series*

LEFT BELOW *Geoff Duke leaps over Ballaugh Bridge on his 500 cc BMW during the 1958 Senior TT. His partnership with the German machine was never a prolific one*

RIGHT *Helmut Fath, one of sidecar racing's all time greats shared in BMW's success. The picture shows him in the Isle of Man in 1959 with a typical Clypse Course backdrop*

BSA

The story of BSA's world championship career is more one of what might have been!

Their successes during the 50's were restricted mainly to the domestic scene and not in Europe but in 1953 Geoff Duke was allowed to test ride a 250 cc horizontal single cylinder twin-carb dohc racer which never saw the light of day.

Duke said the machine had great potential and that its handling was first class which obviously delighted designer Doug Hele. But Duke's comments were to be irrelevant as the Small Heath factory's management team prematurely scrapped the project.

They wanted firm guarantees that the bike would be a winner from the word go and with Moto Guzzi and

NSU doing great things in the 250 class at that time those sort of undertakings could not be given.

However tremendous pressure was put on BSA management after Duke had completed some 30 trouble-free laps of Oulton Park, lapping only a couple of seconds outside the lap record without streamlining on the machine.

The MC1 as it was code named within the factory was reputed to be producing 32 bhp at 10,000 revs and could safely be revved to 11,000. Conservative estimates of its top speed without a fairing were 110 mph which compared with 108 for a Manx Norton in the same trim.

Many felt that this was Britain's only chance to win the 250 cc world title or to break the foreign domination of Lightweight TTs. But alas that was not to be.

Instead the role of the BSA racing machine was restricted to helping up and coming riders on their way to the top. Big names like Bob McIntyre, Derek Minter and Phil Read all cut their teeth on BSAs in Clubmans racing.

The title 'clubmans' would have no significance in modern racing circles—a network of grass roots racing

LEFT *Cadwell Park action with Dickie Dale putting his BSA racer through its paces on the Mountain*

BELOW *A brace of 'Goldies' in the winners' enclosure as Alastair King (left) and Ben Denton shake hands after the 1954 Senior Clubmans TT*

events which may or may not throw up future talent but in the 1950's the Clubmans TT was a sure guide as to the future of any rider.

The best known model is the Gold Star which took its name from a memorable day at Brooklands in 1937. Any rider who could lap the Surrey banked circuit at over 100 mph during a race was awarded a Gold Star. Walter Handley excelled himself that day and got round at 107.57 christening the model which was to become the Birmingham company's most famous product.

His fastest lap, which incidentally was part of a race winning performance, came on an Empire Star but the model was re-named Gold Star in recognition of his achievement.

Prior to the Second World War the 'Goldie' took the form of a 500 but when it was re-introduced after the war it was a 350 model later to be followed by a 500 version.

Development continued at Small Heath and in 1954 a new engine design was unveiled. Power output was improved giving the 350 30 bhp and its bigger capacity stable mate 37 bhp.

Most of BSA's racing successes came in the prestigious Clubmans TTs of the 50's. In fact so dependent were they for success from that race at the Isle of Man that when the event was dropped BSA faded out of the limelight for the remainder of the decade.

Off the domestic scene BSA did record successes at the famous Daytona races. Bobby Hill won the 1954 big race for the factory.

ABOVE *Peter Davey was one of scores of British riders who chose BSA for their 1950s racing efforts*

BELOW *1956 action from Crystal Palace with R. W. Baksh showing the way on his 348 cc Gold Star*

DKW

Like their fellow Germans BMW, the DKW factory had to pick up the threads of production after the consequences of a world war. Their original plant at Zschopau was in Russian occupied territory when peace was declared and so they had to relocate their activities in Ingolstadt, West Germany, and start all over again.

Zschopau in Saxony continued its life as MZ and the two factories were to become arch rivals in grand prix competition during the 1950's.

It was not until 1953 that the name of DKW was seen in world championship racing (this was two years after the Germans were re-admitted to the FIM). Before the war DKW had been at the top of the tree in lightweight racing with their supercharged split singles and split twins but once again the change in the supercharging rules forced a big re-think by DKW designers.

The factory's first post-war offering was an inclined 125 cc single and that was followed by a 250 cc twin by a simple process of doubling up. It was on this machine that Siegfried Wunsche finished third in the 1953 250 cc Lightweight TT.

But it was to be in the 350 cc class that DKW were to achieve most satisfaction with a unique three cylinder layout.

One of the driving forces behind DKW's development in the 50s was Helmut Görg and he headed the team which designed the three cylinder 350 cc bike which was to achieve 45 bhp at 9700 rpm.

The strange layout in which the outer cylinders were near-vertical and the middle one horizontal presented some problems over firing intervals but a workable system was achieved by setting the crank-pins on the outside cylinder at 120 degrees and the centre crank pin 45 degrees out of phase with the right-hand one.

The initial power output was 31 bhp and Wunsche rode in the Jnr TT of 1953 only to retire. Only two years after taking over development of the machine Görg's brilliance had found an extra 14 bhp which gave the machine a top speed of 140 mph and an incredible fuel consumption of 30 mpg.

One of the very canny things the development engineers incorporated in the machine was a rev

One of DKW's most successful riders, Siegfried Wunsche of Germany, pictured on the amazing three cylinder 350 cc machine

counter which registered the peak of revs achieved on any particular run. And this reading could not be wiped out unless a magnet was used.

The engine would rev quite freely to 15,000 but the safe limit was 11,000. Unless the test rider carried a magnet around with him there was no way he could disguise a slip of the throttle hand.

One of DKW's best world championship results came in 1955 when works rider August Hobl finished third in the 350 title chase. The following year he was runner-up in the class. Unfortunately that was DKW's final year in competition.

Although they didn't win a world title during their short reign in world championship racing their presence was highly respected by other factories. Their chief rivals at that time were Moto Guzzi and their team manager, Fergus Anderson, a former motor cycling world champion himself confessed that it was only the brilliance of his pilot Bill Lomas which thwarted DKW's efforts at the time.

LEFT *Karl Lottes and his 250 DKW at Scarborough in 1955*

BELOW *The 350 cc DKW with its unique cylinder layout. Head of development in the 1950s, Helmut Görg, squeezed 140 mph from the machine*

Cecil Sandford rode the 350 DKW ; here he is pictured on his way to fourth place in the 1956 350 cc TT

Ducati

Financially backed by the unlikely combination of the Italian government and the Vatican, the Ducati factory did not return to production after the war until the 1950's and their chances of world championship success were greatly improved when they hired Ing. Fabio Taglioni in 1954.

It was Taglioni who designed the now world famous desmodromic head a system of controlling valve opening and closing by means of separate cams and one which allowed very high revs without the fear of wrecking valve gear.

This positive valve control mechanism first appeared on a racing machine at the Swedish Grand Prix in 1956 in the hands of Degli Antoni and to say that he won the 125 cc race convincingly would be a bit of an under statement—he lapped every other rider!

Just to prove that their grand prix debut was no fluke the Bologna factory that year sent riders Fargas and Ralachs to the Barcelona 24 hour race and won the 125 cc class. This was a clear illustration that Ducati had developed a machine capable of high speed and reliability.

The following year Ducati concentrated on road bike production (racing doesn't directly create revenue!) but just to maintain their presence in the racing world they sent Bruno Spaggiari and Alberto Gandossi to

Barcelona and once again they were victorious in their class.

Serious world championship racing began for Ducati at the 1958 TT where Romolo Ferri, Dave Chadwick and Sammy Miller finished second, third and fourth respectively behind the ever impressive Carlo Ubbiali on an MV.

Swiss star Luigi Taveri who had led the TT until he retired, couldn't stop Ubbiali scoring yet another world championship win in the Dutch TT. Taveri finished second and Gandossi fourth. Taveri's consolation was that he finished just a short head behind the victor and set a new lap record.

Ducati's grand prix breakthrough came in Belgium at Spa the following weekend where Gandossi, Ferri, Chadwick and Taveri finished first, second, fourth and sixth respectively.

In Germany Ducati had a disasterous time. They were leading the race but Ferri crashed, Gandossi's bike broke down and Taveri's engine went sick. In

RIGHT *Ducati gave Mike Hailwood his first classic victory. Pictured here on his way to winning the 1959 125 cc Ulster Grand Prix he set record speeds*

BELOW *The beautiful 250 cc Ducati twin as it appeared at the 1956 Milan Show. It didn't feature in world championship results*

Sweden the factory recorded a one-two thanks to Taveri and Gandossi. The best MV-mounted Ubbiali could manage this time was third.

As the world championship chase went to Dundrod, scene of the Ulster Grand Prix, Ducati were looking strong candidates for the 1958 125 cc world championship. But that was not to be!

Gandossi was leading the title chase and indeed was leading the race when he fell, letting in Ubbiali to snatch victory. Gandossi remounted to cross the line fourth but that was to be the costliest crash of the Italian's career. Team mates Taveri and Chadwick separated him from the victor.

The last race of the 1958 season was to provide Ducati with their most satisfying result. The scene was Monza, the event the Italian Grand Prix and of all the races in the year the Italian factories wanted to do well on their home ground.

The Bologna men slaughtered MV, taking the first five places. Their heroes were Spagiarri, Gandossi, Francesco Villa, Chadwick and Taveri in that order. The world championship season was over and MV had once again clinched the 125 cc world title. How

The highly successful 125 cc Ducati. This close-up shows the desmodromic head, which allowed high revs with safety

frustrated Ducati must have been to know that all that lay between them and the title was Gandossi's fall in Ireland!

Ducati sent another partnership to the Barcelona endurance race again in 1958 and Mandolini and Maranghi came away with the almost habitual class victory.

Apart from the desmodromic head arrangement Ducati's engines were very standard in appearance. One could even see where the kick-start would have been accommodated on their grand prix motors!

The factory technicians did become a little more adventurous for that memorable grand prix at Monza in 1958. Third man home Villa rode an experimental twin cylinder machine which pushed out 22.2 bhp at 14,000 rpm with a speed of 118 mph. However as with many brilliant European designs it didn't see the light of day.

The following season Bruno Spaggiari injured himself and the factory decided later that year to pull out of world championship racing despite that fact that they had a four cylinder machine on the chocks as well as their twin.

Britain's most famous racing son, the late Mike Hailwood had fond memories of the 125 cc Ducati for its was in 1959 at the Ulster Grand Prix, riding such a machine that he recorded his first ever classic win.

Later 250 and 350 parallel twins were introduced, one of which was for Hailwood, but the factory decided to wind up its racing activities.

Mike Hailwood's formative years revolved around the 125 cc Ducati. Here he is pictured on his way to third spot in the 1959 TT

Gilera

One of the most exciting and successful marques seen on the grand prix circuits of the 1950's had to be that of the 500 cc Gilera, which in eight years of racing won a total of 31 grands prix.

The post-war breakthrough came at the 1950 Belgian Grand Prix when Umberto Masetti won on the four cylinder Gilera. This was to be the first of many grand prix victories which were to lead to six individual world titles and five manufacturers awards in the years leading up to Gilera's withdrawal from racing in 1957.

The four cylinder machines, later to become affectionately known as the 'fire engines' because of their bright red livery, were troublesome at first. Given its debut in 1949 the multi proved difficult to handle and for some of those early races in the 50s the factory relied on the tried and tested single cylinder 'Saturno'.

Masetti went on to win the 1950 500 cc world championship after a season-long struggle with Geoff Duke on the Norton. The following season, with Duke benefitting from the superior handling of the 'feather-bed' Norton he managed to beat the Gilera challenge

but the following year the Italians were back on top again.

Duke had been approached by the Italians on several occasions before he finally decided to abandon his patriotism in 1953 and join Gilera. As the British factories resources dwindled Duke realised that he was wasting his time and agreed to the transfer.

What an impact Duke made on the Italian factory's world championship efforts. Within three years of joining the factory he had completed a hat-trick of 500 cc world titles for them though a half-season suspension spoiled his chances in 1956.

At the time he joined the Arcore factory Piero Taruffi, the man who won them their first important race, the Tripoli Grand Prix in 1939, was development engineer. He and Duke struck up a good relationship and through Duke's deep understanding of handling

On his way to victory in the 1955 Senior TT, Geoff Duke wrestles the mighty four cylinder Gilera over Ballaugh Bridge

ABOVE *Skilfully using the clutch, Geoff Duke rounds the Mountside Hairpin at Olivers Mount in 1955 on his 500 Gilera*

RIGHT *Astride the 350 cc Gilera at Monza in 1956, Geoff Duke is pictured with Signor Ferruccio Gilera, son of the Mr Gilera!*

problems on racing machines he soon had the powerful fours in perfect race order.

Duke may well have scored another championship win before his employers pulled out of competition in 1957 but injury dogged his chances.

Spurred on by their dominance in the 500 cc class Gilera, under the supervision of Count Guiseppe Gilera, who controlled the factory's operations until just a year before his death, at the age of 84, in 1971, wheeled out 125 and 350 sisters to the powerful 500 cc-four.

In 1956, their debut year, the smaller of the two newcomers first appeared at the Belgian Grand Prix where Romolo Ferri crossed the line third. His mount incorporated several of the successful features introduced on the 500 machine. There were telescopic front forks and a rear swinging arm unit.

The twin cylinder dohc engine with a six speed gearbox produced 20 bhp at 12,000 rpm by the time it had won the German Grand Prix, complete with full fairing and finished second at the Ulster Grand Prix.

Quite amazingly the factory then lost interest in the 125 class and the machine was put in moth balls and

ABOVE *Oulton Park 1956 and Reg Armstrong on a 500 Gilera*

BELOW *Geoff Duke at La Source hairpin, Spa in 1956, on the 500 Gilera*

never seen again despite its very creditable opening series of races.

The 350 was a direct descendent of the 500 and it won its first outing at the 1956 Italian Grand Prix at Monza where Gilera's involvement in sidecar racing continued to thrive with a win.

So with some satisfactory results behind them in 1956, although they didn't win a world title, Gilera looked forward to great things in 1957.

With Duke back in action again and teaming up with Libero Liberati the prospects looked exciting. But it was out of the frying pan and into the fire for Duke. Having returned to his old form he crashed heavily at Imola just before the 1957 TT and picked up a shoulder injury which was to keep him out of racing long enough not to get a top three classification in either 350 or 500 cc world championships.

On Duke's recommendation Gilera signed Bob McIntyre for the rest of the year and what a piece of advice that turned out to be from Duke. In his first major assignment for them, the Isle of Man TT races, he won both Junior and Senior races and set the first 100 mph lap of the Mountain course.

Liberati went to take the 1957 500 cc world title but both he and McIntyre could not hold off hard Australian

Keith Campbell, in his first and last season for Moto Guzzi, taking the 350 title from McIntyre by eight points.

Sadly 1957 was to be the last year of competition for Gilera. For economic reasons they, along with Moto Guzzi and FB Mondial, withdrew from racing, shocking the grand prix world.

Gilera's successes were not restricted to the solo classes. They also experienced widespread success on three wheels during the 1950's.

During the opening four years of the world championships Gilera finished runner-up each time in the sidecar class thanks to the efforts of Ercole Frigerio and Albino Milani.

Although 1957 was Gilera's grand prix swansong the machines were used in the November of that year to have a crack at the world speed records. Romolo Ferri set a new one hour record for 125 machines, McIntyre set a new target for allcomers at 141.37 miles and that was on a 350 cc Gilera, and Albino Milani broke the sidecar one hour record, covering a distance of 134.4 miles.

McIntyres amazing mileage at Monza stood until Mike Hailwood broke it at Daytona on a 500 cc MV Agusta in 1964!

ABOVE *Golden Jubilee TT winner Bob McIntyre on the Gilera*
BELOW *Phil Read and Derek Minter were Gilera users*

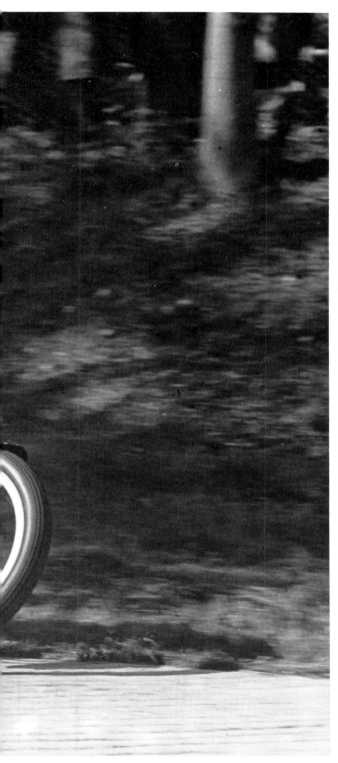

Guzzi

If anyone has any doubts as to whether Moto Guzzi is one of the most successful racing factories of all time they should just digest their impressive list of achievements.

When they retired from racing at the end of 1957 along with their fellow Italian manufacturers they had won 3327 international races, set 134 world speed records, taken 47 Italian championships, won 55 national titles, won 11 TT's and most important of all had won 14 world championships (eight individual, six manufacturers').

Their introduction to grand prix racing had been made against a background of frustration. In 1948 their Italian works rider Omobono Tenni had a gaping lead in the Senior TT after the fourth lap but the 120 degree V-twin, basically a 13-year-old design, went onto one cylinder and he coasted home in ninth spot. The following year Britain's Bob Foster was leading the Senior on a similar machine when his clutch gave way! The lack of results did not deter the Italian engineers. They could sense victory was just around the corner. The power output was transformed from 42 bhp at 6800 rpm to 48 bhp at 8000 rpm. As a result the bike had many good placings but only one win at the 1951 Swiss Grand Prix.

Now disillusioned, the factory took the step of dropping the model at the end of 1951.

If the 500 cc design team were down in the mouth that certainly was not the case with the 250 cc back-up crew. Quite simply their machine was the most successful in its class during those first years of the world championships.

The single cylinder machine, by 1952 was turning out 27 bhp at 7500 rpm and won its races not only because of its power but because of its great handling qualities—the petrol tank was even tailor-made to accommodate the rider's arms.

Capable of 109 mph the 'Gambalunghino' (little long leg) so called because of its unusually long stroke (bore and stroke 68 × 68 mm) won the lightweight TTs of 1949, 51, 52 and 53 and the 250 world titles in 1949, 51 and 52. Moto Guzzi were held at bay in 1950 by the brilliance of Dario Ambrosini and his Benelli. Ambrosini was killed in 1951 and this greatly helped Guzzi to retain their supremacy.

At that time chief designer at the Moto Guzzi factory at Mandello del Lario, on the eastern shores of Lake

The beauty of a 1954 Moto Guzzi racer captured at Cadwell Park.
The Italian factory is one of the most successful ever

Como, was Giulio Carcano and he decided that to regain his factory's pride in the 500 cc class four cylinders were necessary. So an in-line four with shaft drive and water-cooling was produced. The bike also featured an advanced dohc mechanism and fuel injection. It had been seen during practice at Monza but was not wheeled out in earnest until the 1953 season.

The bike had a fairytale winning debut at Hockenheim in the hands of Enrico Lorenzetti but ironically was soon to be scrapped because of its almost total unreliability after that glorious opening.

But, as always, things were looking bright in the smaller classes. By now Fergus Anderson, that articulate Scot, was in the Guzzi line-up and after victorious rides in the 1952–53 lightweight TT's he persuaded Carcano to build a 350 version of the 'Gambalunghino'.

The first 350 Moto Guzzi was in fact only a 320 cc. Despite the capacity deficiency Anderson rode it to third place in the 1953 Junior TT and followed it up with a win at Hockenheim. Naturally Carcano was impressed and mid-season a true 350 was produced

ABOVE *1956 Junior TT winner Ken Kavanagh pictured at Governors Bridge on the 350 Moto Guzzi*

RIGHT ABOVE *Arthur Wheeler, one of the Italian factory's best remembered riders, on his way to eighth place in the 1957 250 cc TT*

RIGHT BELOW *Dickie Dale on the sensational 500 cc Guzzi V8 in the 1957 Senior TT. One of the most exotic pieces of raceware ever*

pushing the power output from 28.5 bhp at 8400 rpm to 31 bhp at 7700 rpm. Anderson went on to win the 1953 350 world title on the new addition to the Guzzi stable, and with the power increased to 33.5 bhp at 7500 rpm on the following year's model he repeated his achievement, while NSU remained dominant in the 250 title chase, formerly easy meat for Guzzi.

Much of the increase in speed of the revised machines was down to the factory's research into streamlining. Guzzi were first to use the famous 'dustbin' fairing which was moulded only after many weeks in the wind tunnel perfecting the shape.

This innovation came during the 1953 season and

LEFT ABOVE *The amazing Guzzi V8 had tiny cylinder measurements of 41 × 41 mm, eight 20 mm carburettors and eight short exhaust pipes*

LEFT *Side view of the complex Guzzi V8 power unit. With Keith Campbell in charge it was clocked at 178 mph in Belgium!*

ABOVE *Australian Keith Campbell doing his stuff for Motor Guzzi at the 1957 TT, the factory's last year of competition*

there is no doubt that the invention greatly assisted Anderson on his way to consecutive world crowns in 1953–54.

In 1955 Carcano had increased the power of the 350 to 35 bhp at 7800 rpm and his brilliance had produced a space frame designed specially to accommodate the 'dustbin' fairings. This time Bill Lomas was the first string rider and he was to win the title easily for the coming two seasons. In 1957 Guzzi again triumphed but this time it was with the help of hard-riding Australian Keith Campbell. Of course 1957, as with Gilera and FB Mondial, marked the end of an era for Motor Guzzi as they withdrew from world championship competition.

The V-8 remains today as one of the most exotic pieces of raceware ever produced. Designed by Carcano the machine was basically a 90 degree V-8 with tiny cylinder measurements of 44 × 41 mm. There were eight 20 mm carburettors and eight short exhaust pipes. The water-cooled machine was enough to psyche out any rider on the grid!

The engine was mounted transversely in the frame and despite all its gadgetry the whole thing only weighed in at 320 lb.

In 1956 the machine was said to be kicking out 62 bhp at 12,000 rpm. This meant that the bike was capable of 162 mph 24 years ago!

But by the time Campbell got hold of it it was producing 75 bhp and combined with a 'dustbin' fairing this made for record speeds. At Spa the Australian was clocked at 178 mph on the Masta Straight.

Looking back on Moto-Guzzi's world championship achievements they were undoubtedly enhanced by the advantageous power-to-weight ratios which Carcano and his team were able to come up with.

The 350 weighed only 216 lb and the 500 just 20 lb more, the early 120 degree twin (1935) had only tipped the scales at 375 lb.

Matchless

The Matchless G45 racer is a machine everyone remembers. It has the same ring to it as the Manx Norton or the AJS 7R. First appearing in 1953 it reigned for five years and was then replaced with the G50 single-knocker single but its real roots go back to 1951 when a twin cylinder 500 cc Matchless appeared at the Manx Grand Prix.

The AMC racing department had developed a 500 cc twin based on the G9 touring machine. Robin Sherry rode the machine at the 1951 Manx and sent everyone home happy by finishing fourth behind a trio of tried and tested Nortons.

The Plumstead race shop worked for the next 12 months to build a machine capable of winning the Manx Grand Prix and their goal was achieved as Derek Farrant set new race and lap records with a start to finish victory in 1952.

These two years had been pure experimentation but with two very successful visits to the Isle of Man behind them Matchless decided to start producing a purpose built 500 cc racer. Enter the G45 in 1953! During the five years the machine was sold its performance was steadily improved. By 1956 the bike was producing 48 bhp at 7200 rpm.

In 1959 the G45 was dropped in favour of the single cylinder G50, designed by AMC's ace engineer Jack Williams. It was derived from the highly successful 350 7R racer and at first there were many similarities like 7R valves. But these were later replaced with purpose built valves.

LEFT *Bob McIntyre prepares for the start of the 1953 Senior TT with his Matchless. Greater days in the Isle of Man were to come*

LEFT BELOW *Frank Perris on a G50 Matchless passes through Parliament Square, Ramsey, during the 1956 Senior TT*

BELOW *A packed crowd at Cadwell Park watch a Matchless exponent putting his machine through its paces at the entrance to Hall Bends. The Matchless enjoyed good sales through easy maintenance*

LEFT *Ready for the off! A senior TT competitor warms up his machine for the 1956 event*

BELOW LEFT *A battle for supremacy among the British. Jack Brett (Norton) chases Derek Ennett (Matchless) at the 1956 TT*

BELOW *The new Matchless G50, successor to the G45, being put through its paces at Brands Hatch in October 1958*

Though derived from the 7R, and perhaps would have been more appropriately christened an AJS the G50 was marketed under the Matchless banner.

Many were bemused as to why AMC chose to go from a proven twin cylinder machine to a single for their new model in 1959 but their thinking had in many ways been influenced by practicality and convenience for the racing enthusiast.

The big single pumped out 47 bhp at 7200 rpm and although it was slightly slower than its nearest rival the Manx Norton its simple chain driven single cam engine was easier to tune and maintain.

For this reason it became very popular with the private owner and obviously boosted AMC's sales. Between 1959 and 1963, when the model was dropped, the company sold 180 of the machines.

Mondial

Until the 1950s 125 cc racing had not earned the widespread respect from other racing quarters which it would have liked and it was the engineering wizardry of the Italian FB Mondial factory which was to finally achieve that respect for the ultra-lightweight class.

Mondial reigned from 1949 to 1957 and enjoyed their most successful years at the beginning of the decade. They were 125 cc world champions in 1949, 1950 and 1951. So prolific were the machines which Alfonso Drusiani designed—dohc singles—that they were a match for many larger machines, much to the embarrassment of their rival factories. Indeed it was this fact which helped establish the new-found credibility for the class.

Their reign at the beginning of the decade came to an end in 1952 with the arrival of the 125 cc MV. There was little to shout about from then until 1956 when the factory fielded redesigned racers and re-established their supremacy in the 250 class as well as the 125 category. In 1957 they scooped the 125 and 250 world titles and the manufacturer's awards in both classes and Britain's Cecil Sandford had the distinction of becoming the factory's only 250 world champion.

Along with Moto-Guzzi and Gilera, Mondial withdrew from world championship competition at the end of 1957. But after their retirement Mike Hailwood rode a privately entered Mondial with distinction in the 250 class.

ABOVE *A 125 cc Mondial racer pictured at the 1956 TT. By this time their former world champion Carlo Ubbiali had changed camps and was winning for MV, the rival Italian factory*

RIGHT *On his winning way at the 1956 Hutchinson 100 at Silverstone is Cecil Sandford on a 250 Mondial*

BELOW *1951 125 cc world champion Carlo Ubbiali on a Mondial*

ABOVE LEFT *The sleek lines of the 125 cc Mondial in the hands of Tarquinio Provini on his way to TT victory in 1957*

LEFT *Cecil Sandford (29) and Sammy Miller on 250 Mondials in the 1957 TT. Miller took fourth place with Sandford in fifth*

ABOVE *Mondial ace Tarquinio Provini on his way to victory in the 1957 125 cc TT held on the Clypse Course*

BELOW *1959 TT action with Mike Hailwood on the 250 Mondial chasing Tarquinio Provini who by then had changed camps to MV*

Morini

This Italian factory's world championship pedigree is a sketchy one. The machine first appeared in 125 form in the 1948 Italian championship. It won the prestigious series and in consequence appeared in the first year of the world championships in 1949 when R. Magi finished runner-up to Nello Pagani on a Mondial and his team mate Umberto Masetti finished third. Those early machines were single cylinder four strokes with a massive finned engine and a chain driven overhead camshaft.

Emilio Mendogni drew first blood for his factory at Monza in 1952 and he scored a second grand prix victory for Morini in Spain the same year. Despite his efforts he could only manage third overall in that year's 125 cc title chase. The following year Morini finished second at Monza but their interest in the world championships was waning. That Monza appearance was to be the last for the 125. The factory engineers were to concentrate their efforts on the 175 cc production racer from then on. In 1957 Morini returned to world championship racing with a 250 cc single. Its debut was a frustrating one for the factory, retiring while well placed at Monza. By the following season the machine had been revamped and Mendogni and

Giampiero Zubani ran rings round the MV Agustas of Carlo Ubbiali and Tarquinio Provini at Monza.

When the 250 first arrived on the scene its dohc engine was producing 30 bhp at 10,000 rpm but by the time the development engineers had finished their job they had managed to squeeze 36 bhp from it with peak power coming at 10,500 rpm.

Morini's most noted rider was Provini who finished third for the factory in the 1960 TT. During the two years prior to that their best result was their emphatic win in the 1958 Italian Grand Prix at Monza.

RIGHT *The inimitable Tarquinio Provini flat out on the 250 Morini. He got the best out of the Italian factory's machine*

BELOW *Pictured on its debut in 1957 the 250 cc Morini which was well placed at Monza before retiring. Next year it ran rings around the MVs at the same meeting*

LEFT *Close-up of the 250 cc dohc Morini racer which scored an emphatic win at the Italian Grand Prix at Monza in 1958*

BELOW LEFT *Like so many of the Italian racers of the 1950s the Moto Morini had a certain stylish aggression for that period*

BELOW *A look inside the 175 cc power unit which Morini engineers concentrated on when their 125 cc efforts waned towards the middle of the decade*

MV Agusta

What sets Meccanica Verghera Agusta apart from the other Italian factories is that it did not chose to withdraw from world championship racing at the end of 1957. For this reason the factory has always had to live with the accusation that it clinched much of its early success cheaply. Nevertheless they went on to achieve an almost incomparable record during the 1950s—82 classic victories and 15 world championships! In fact MV have won more 500 cc world titles than any other factory since world championship records began.

Although known best for their 500 cc efforts MV's story begins in the late 1940s when the massive Societa Construzioni Aeronautiche Giovanni Agusta, decided to develop a sideline. Until this time they had been involved solely in aviation work but between 1945, when the decision was taken to build motorcycles, until the end of the decade, more than 15 different designs had been produced. The first racing machines, which were 125 cc two-strokes, appeared in the Italian championships in 1948 and then the following year their world championship debut came at Monza where modest seventh to twelfth positions were

achieved. But MV have always been renowned for their brilliant four-stroke work and it was in 1950 that the first of a long line of such products was to leave the Gallarate factory.

The man behind the design of the first four cylinder four stroke was Ing. Pietro Remor who joined MV from the rival Italian Gilera camp.

Within five months of changing jobs Remor had a 500 cc grand prix racer ready for testing. The first of a long line of beautiful-sounding machines had a bore and stroke of 54 × 54 mm with the cylinders set across the frame and a four speed gearbox to transfer the

ABOVE RIGHT *Heading for third place in the 1957 TT, Luigi Taveri on the 125 cc MV. Action was on the Clypse Course that year*

BELOW RIGHT *In his first year of racing Mike Hailwood on a 125 cc MV at the Olivers Mount circuit, Scarborough*

BELOW *The 1957 MV Augusta four. This was the machine on which John Surtees completely dominated grand prix racing until the end of the decade*

50 bhp to the road. Peak power was at 10,000 rpm and the machine could be geared for a top speed of 129 mph.

First grand prix for the new MV was the Belgian in 1950 when Italian rider Arturo Artesiani finished a creditable fifth. From then until the end of the season its best performance was third in the Italian grand prix.

Remor had also been commissioned to build a four stroke 125 cc racer and that made its debut at the 1951 TT. Its first race was not quite as successful as that of its bigger sister but then again it could be argued that the Isle of Man is a somewhat more demanding course for newcomers!

In fact the 37¾ miles of varying gradients had little to

LEFT *Setting off along Glencrutchery Road. John Surtees starts his final TT on a 500 MV*

RIGHT *Italian Carlo Ubbiali at Governors Bridge in the 1959 125 cc TT. This year his MV could only take him to fifth place*

BELOW *On his way to victory in the 500 cc class at the 1958 Ulster Grand Prix is John Surtees on the mighty MV*

do with the 125's demise—it seized halfway down Bray Hill on the opening lap! The 500 managed two laps before it completed the misery for the factory engineers.

MV had already recognised their need for a rider with the capability of transmitting information from the track to the back-up crew. Someone who could analyse what was happening while he was flat on the tank and relay that in technical jargon on his return to the pits.

That man was the late Les Graham whose first full season with the factory was in 1951. When Graham first went to the factory he found the 500, which he was to ride, needed masses of development work carrying out on it. That first year brought little in the way of rewards as he found the handling poor, gear selection hit and miss and the bike being outpaced by the rival Gileras.

Big changes were made for the following year mainly on Graham's recommendation. Having been shaft driven in 1951 the following year's machine was converted to chain drive. A fifth gear was added and the exhaust pipes siamezed on both sides. The telescopic front fork was exchanged for an Earls type pivoted fork with better damping.

Graham's suggestions soon transformed the performance of the machine. In 1952 at the TT he was lying second to Geoff Duke's Norton after four laps and went on to finish runner-up to Reg Armstrong's Norton, despite losing 800 revs from a missed gear. This also penalised him with an over-long pit stop.

There was more excitement for the MV camp later that summer when Graham led the Ulster Grand Prix only to be forced to retire with no tread left on his rear tyre. The problem was another niggling symptom in the evolution of the machine. There wasn't enough clearance between the rear mudguard and the tyre and the notorious bumps on the Clady circuit's seven mile straight took their toll.

But there had to be an end to the misfortune with such a hard-working team. Graham won the final two grands prix of 1952 for the Italians, in Italy and in Spain.

It was the major breakthrough they had been waiting for and the achievement was even more creditable in that he rode for the last 20 of the 48 laps at Barcelona on three cylinders—one plug lead had come adrift. What a testimony as to the skill of the Englishman!

So as 1953 arrived the MV team were turning the corner in their development programme but little did they know that tragedy was to strike that year at the TT robbing them of one of the greatest names ever to be associated with their marque!

It was at the start of the second lap of the Senior TT when Graham was killed on Bray Hill. He was trailing leader Geoff Duke when he met his death and that marked the end of a brilliant career. The irony of the incident was that Graham had just scored his first TT victory on an MV in the 125 cc race.

Obviously the factory was knocked for six at the loss of Graham. The 500 was only used from time to time for the rest of that year and the 125 went on to record victories in Germany and Spain to tie for the manufacturers award with NSU on points. A time tie-break gave them that coveted award by 35.8s!

In 1954 the factory continued the development of their 500 and 350 cc models but with little success despite much experimentation with streamlining and the inclusion of a six speed gearbox.

In addition to the right sort of development work the factory definitely needed to find a replacement for Graham as close to his calibre as possible. They looked to Rhodesian Ray Amm for this but tragically his association with them was to last less than a race. He was killed on his first appearance on an MV in a non-championship race at Imola while riding the four cylinder 350 model. With no top class rider for the remainder of that season MV had to bow down to the superiority of the Geoff Duke/Gilera combination.

Their consolation that year came in the 125 class where Carlo Ubbiali convincingly clinched the world title. In fact MV won all six grands prix in that class that year.

The factory continued their successful run in the 125 class in 1956 and were all conquering at 250 level as well with their twin and single cylinder machines. Ubbiali and Luigi Taveri were the riders and Ubbiali had a marvellous season completing a 125 and 250 cc double for his employers.

At 350 and 500 level MV had found their long-awaited Messiah—John Surtees. In his first year he won MV their first Senior TT and indeed their first 500 cc world title and that was just the shape of things to come.

Like Graham, Surtees was an intelligent articulate rider who was able to liaise perfectly with his back up crew. Apart from Gilera's final world championship season in 1957, Surtees and MV were to dominate 350 and 500 cc racing until the end of the decade.

In 1958, 59 and 60 Surtees won both classes each year and in those same years Ubbiali and Tarquinio Provini had a stranglehold on the 125 and 250 classes for the factory.

Eventual winner of the 1959 250 cc TT, Tarquinio Provini (25) chases MV team mate Carlo Ubbiali at Ballacraine

MZ

The name MZ was born after the Second World War
when the DKW factory at Zschopau found itself in
Russian occupied territory. The factory of the original
name decided to re-locate itself in West Germany but life
went on at Zschopau under the MZ banner. Motorrader-
werk Zschopau continued DKW's involvement in the
production of two-stroke motor cycles and its chances
of world championship success took a giant leap forward
when designer Walter Kaaden joined them in 1952.
His name was to become world famous for his influence on the future of two-stroke design. His first
racer appeared in 1953 and was a single cylinder, three
speed 125. But the major point of interest was the disc
valve induction a feature which would recur in all
future MZ models.

That first machine produced 13 bhp at 8000 rpm.
By 1955 Kaaden had doubled-up the 125 power unit
into a successful 250 twin. That same year he ex-
perimented successfully with expansion chamber
design and squeezed an extra two bhp from the 250.

The final stages of development before the machine
was thrust into serious grand prix competition were

*German Ernst Degner in action for the MZ factory in the 125 cc TT
at Governors Bridge in 1959*

*Action from the Clypse Course at the Isle of Man in 1959 as Ernst
Degner flashes past the Manx Arms at Onchan on the 125 MZ*

ABOVE *Gary Hocking had a good day at the 1959 Ulster Grand Prix. Pictured en route for 250 victory he was second in the 125 race—both for MZ*

ABOVE LEFT *Luigi Taveri on his way to what should have been a 125 cc TT victory for MZ. But his helmet tightened and he slowed for second*

BELOW LEFT *Gary Hocking (MZ) leads Mike Hailwood (Ducati) during the 125 cc Ulster Grand Prix. It was to be Hailwood's first GP win*

building in a six speed gearbox and the addition of coil ignition to give consistency in the ingition system.

First news of the MZ in world championship results came when Ernst Degner crossed the line 10th in the 1956 125 cc German Grand Prix but they had to wait until 1958 at Hockenheim until they got their first grand prix victory again in the 125 cc class. The same season saw their 250 cc breakthrough in Sweden. Now MZ were a real threat to world championship honours but there was one major factor working against them!

Despite having some big names associated with them during the 1950s, like Rhodesian Gary Hocking and Luigi Taveri, who finished second in the 1959 125 cc TT, the factory were unable to pay big fees to their riders and this of course worked against them.

That second place for Taveri in the Isle of Man could so easily have been the most famous victory for the East Germans. He was leading the race quite comfortably when a tight crash helmet began giving him double vision and he had to ease the pace allowing Tarquinio Provini to take honours for MV.

Rhodesian Gary Hocking, with a record speed and record lap, won the 1959 250 cc Ulster Grand Prix for the East Germans

Norton

Norton is definitely one of the greatest names in road racing with no less than 34 TT victories to its credit.

The factory resumed life after the Second World War on a very confident note with all its major rivals having to review their activities in the light of the outlawing of supercharging. Norton had never delved into this field of development and so they had an easy job in those immediate post-war years but it was the return of the manufacturers, who were caught out, which served as the real springboard to Norton's successes during the 1950s.

During the pre-war years Norton had taken a drubbing from the blown Gileras and BMWs at 500 cc level and Velocette and the blown DKW in the 350 class. When peace returned Norton carried on with modified pre-war machines and the expertise of Harold Daniell, Artie Bell, Ernie Lyons and Johnny Lockett.

The combination of an adequate machine and determined riders had been enough to keep them on top but by 1949 the others were catching up again. In 1949 Norton won the Senior TT but that was all.

At the 1949 Italian Grand Prix at Monza the AJS Porcupine, Gilera and Moto Guzzi simply outsped them and Norton couldn't get in the top six. It was an ominous sign of what would happen in 1950 if Norton's design team didn't come up with something special!

While all this alarm was occurring on the world championship scene, Irish racing brothers Rex and Cromie McCandless had been experimenting with a swinging arm frame and they were invited by Norton to help designer Joe Craig to design a new racer.

And so it was that, the new Norton 'featherbed' was born.

The model became known as the 'featherbed' because that was the way Harold Daniell described its handling after his first test ride on the new machine in 1950.

The new frame housed the famous Manx Norton 500 cc power unit which had been introduced in the previous year. The single cylinder engine was to be used until the end of Norton's reign in grand prix racing although plans for twin and four cylinder engines had been on the drawing board.

John Surtees cut his teeth on Nortons. Here he takes the Mere Hairpin at Olivers Mount on a works 500 in 1954

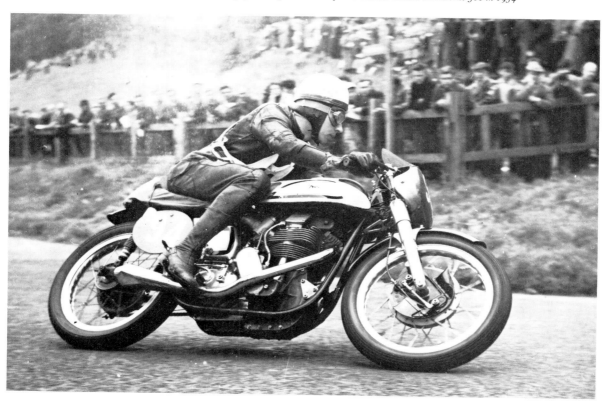

But there was one big aid to Norton's return to competitiveness in 1950 and that was the brilliance of up-and-coming Geoff Duke. He led their return with real flair and recorded a Senior TT victory in 1950 as his employers completed a one-two-three in both Junior and Senior races in the Isle of Man that year.

In 1951 Norton won both manufacturers' world championships (350 and 500 cc) and Duke took the two individual titles. But the following year Umberto Masetti and Gilera relieved them of their 500 cc honours.

Duke's stay with Norton lasted just three seasons. In 1953 after a lot of thinking and demands on his patriotism he decided to leave the British team and join Gilera.

Duke's departure along with that of Reg Armstrong to Gilera brought Ray Amm from Rhodesia and Ken Kavanagh from Australia into the team alongside Englishman Jack Brett. Amm won both TT races in 1953 but for the rest of the world championship programme Norton could not match the superiority of the Italian machines—350 cc Moto Guzzi, 500 cc Gilera.

At this time Kavanagh had been carrying out a test programme for Norton at the Montlhéry track in France. The project concerned the 'kneeler' which was soon to be scrapped but which had some meritorious ideas incorporated into it.

The whole scheme was aimed at getting the aerodynamics of the racing machine right. By getting the rider as low as possible it reduced the frontal area

TT action from 1954 with a typical Isle of Man scene. Much of the factory's world championship success came in sidecars

The Hutchinson 100 in 1956 at Silverstone and the legendary Bob McIntyre is on his way to second place on a Norton

of the machine and therefore the wind resistance. He knelt in a specially designed trough and rested his body on a mattress across the top tubes of the frame.

The whole new concept in frame design meant that pannier fuel tanks had to be built and a pump incorporated to feed the carburettor. The bike used a new 88×82 mm short-stroke engine but sadly the project was to be abandoned in 1954 in the early days of the AMC takeover of Norton.

In fact 1954 was to be Norton's last year in world championship competition. In addition to Ray Amm, Ken Kavanagh and Jack Brett, Syd Lawton was aboard the further-developed single cylinder 500s but he was to be replaced by John Surtees when struck down by injury.

To compensate for scrapping the kneeler project the management allowed more development of the single cylinder power unit to take place. These refinements included the grafting on of a five speed gearbox.

With streamlining refinements these modifications

brought Norton back into the picture a bit more. Amm won the Senior TT and set the fastest lap in the Junior race but apart from winning the Ulster Grand Prix and the Junior and Senior classes at the German Grand Prix there was little joy for the factory.

In 1955 Norton pulled out of world championship racing to concentrate on production of their successful Manx Norton on the home front. They said that grand prix racing was becoming too far removed from the street market. But their official withdrawal was not to mean the end of big names being associated with the marque. Indeed many racing stars were to cut their teeth on Nortons. These included Australians Bob Brown and Jack Ahearn and John Hartle, Frank Perris, Mike Hailwood, Phil Read and more. In the years to come brilliant tuners like Ray Petty, Steve Lancefield and Francis Beart tuned the Manx with great success for men like Hailwood and Derek Minter. But Norton's successes did not only come in the world of solo racing. Equally as impressive at the start of the decade were their world championship sidecar results thanks to the efforts of Eric Oliver and Cyril Smith.

From 1949 to 1953 Norton dominated sidecar racing. Oliver was world champion in the years 1949–50–51–53 and Smith broke his fellow Englishman's hold on the class in 1952.

The Norton supremacy ended when BMW's magnificent reign began in 1954.

ABOVE *Racing Nortons were everywhere in the 1950s. This shot from Cadwell Park in 1956 was typical of the trim they would be raced in*

RIGHT ABOVE *Norton sidecar action from Aintree in 1957 as Jacques Drion and Ingeborg Stoll (96) hold off Bill Beevers and Freddie Fox*

RIGHT BELOW *Two of the greatest Norton exponents. Derek Minter leads John Surtees out of Druids Haripin, Brands Hatch in 1957. Both ride 350s*

RIGHT *Rhodesian Jim Redman used Nortons to catch the eyes of the racing World. Jim is pictured at Brands Hatch in 1958*

BELOW *Scottish favourite Alastair King on his way to sixth place in the 1959 Ulster Grand Prix on a Norton*

NSU

The NSU factory has the distinction of being regarded as the manufacturer to register a quicker impact on world championship road racing than any rival company.

Like many of its fellow manufacturers in war-torn Europe in the late 30s and 40s NSU had the job of rebuilding its factory, at Neckarsulm, in Germany before it could get down to the business of producing motor cycles again. The production centre was completely destroyed by the fighting.

Their pre-war 350 and 500 cc supercharged twins were raced in only German national events because Germany was on probation with the FIM until 1951.

Back in the FIM again the factory made an attack on 125 cc and 250 cc grand prix racing between 1952 and 1955. The 250 works racer was known as the Rennmax and was derived from the ashes of a failure of a 500 cc project which proved too troublesome to persevere with. Developed in 1951 this original engine gave 53 bhp but there were too many teething problems and the project was shelved.

But instead of completely wasting their efforts

factory technicians built a set of crankcases for one of cylinders from the 500 and the single cylinder 125 cc Rennfox was born.

Later the brilliant Dr Walter Froede, who went on to become involved in the Wankel engine project, grafted a couple of cylinders onto another set of existing crankcases and this formed the basis of the Rennmax 250 cc works racer which was to frighten opposition for the next three years.

The Rennmax was given its first serious world championship outing at Monza in September 1952 and it gave Moto Guzzi, who ruled the 250 cc roost at that time, plenty to think about.

Werner Haas rode the machine to second place, only by a short head, behind Enrico Lorenzetti on a Guzzi and Haas forced Scot Fergus Anderson on another Guzzi into third.

With their engines now perfected NSU appeared in

Werner Haas, NSU's brilliant double world champion of the 1950s, pictured on his way to second place in the 1953 125 cc TT

ABOVE *Werner Haas on his way to victory in the 1954 250 cc TT on the unique-looking NSU*

RIGHT *Tucked behind the screen on a 250 NSU at the 1957 Ulster Grand Prix is Irish favourite Tommy Robb*

FAR RIGHT *Mike Hailwood used an NSU Sportsmax for his third place in the 250 cc TT over the Clypse Course in 1958*

PREVIOUS PAGE *The works NSU team prepares to do battle at the French Grand Prix in 1954. They took the first four places in the 250 event!*

1953 with their famous dolphin fairings made out of hammered aluminium. Evidence of their progress came at the 1953 TT when Haas finished second in both 125 and 250 races to Les Graham on an MV and Fergus Anderson on a Guzzi respectively.

At the Dutch TT Haas reversed the orders and for the rest of the season NSU were the factory to watch. In Germany Haas won the 250 race and was second in the 125 class, at the Ulster Grand Prix his achievements were the other way round and then at the Italian Grand Prix he won the 125 race and finished runner up in the 250 race.

That sequence of great results was enough to give Haas both 125 and 250 world championships and he was the first German to do that.

A 250 cc NSU Sportsmax with full fairing. This was the production racer derived from the all-conquering Rennmax

Naturally with such a brilliant 1953 season behind them the factory became even more enthusiastic and by the time the 1954 grand prix season had arrived Froede had increased the power output of the 250 to 33 bhp. The 125 was now kicking out 20 bhp instead of 17.

In the 250 cc TT of that year NSU shattered the opposition. Fielding a much increased team they finished first, second, third, fourth and sixth with the respective efforts of Haas, Rupert Hollaus, Reg Armstrong, Hans-Peter Muller and Hans Baltisberger. In the 125 cc race NSU again came out tops. Hollaus was the winner with Baltisberger fourth.

The rest of the world championship programme was a walkover for the Germans except for the Italian Grand Prix where they did not compete after Hollaus was killed during practice. Hollaus had amassed enough points before his fatal crash to posthumously become 125 cc world champion. Haas was again 250 champion.

After the 1954 Ulster Grand Prix the dolphin fairing was replaced by a full dustbin fairing and this increased the speed of the Rennmax to 135 mph!

In 1955 the factory announced that they were withdrawing from world championship competition. However they would prepare a Sportsmax production 250 model for Hans-Peter Muller to contest the world championship. That move paid off as Muller went on to lift the crown but this was only due to the inconsistency of the Italian factories in the 250 class that season. The Sportsmax remained on the grand prix scene until the turn of the decade and was always the most consistently placed private machine in the series. Among the important names to use the production racer were Mike Hailwood and John Surtees both of whom had great success on the German machine in the 250 class.

Triumph

Although one of the most famous names in the British motor cycle industry the name of Triumph was virtually unknown in grand prix racing during the 1950s.

The story of Triumph's 500 cc racing efforts goes back to 1938 when the famous speed twin was introduced. The machine with the compact vertical twin engine, which retailed at £75, weighed 365 lb and produced 28.5 bhp at 6000 rpm was to have a big bearing on the factory's racing future.

Having set pre-war speed records at Brooklands of 118.02 mph (supercharged 500) and 105.97 (single cylinder 350) Triumph had to re-site their Coventry factory after the war, chosing Meriden as their new home.

Post-war racing enthusiasts who wanted to use Triumph for their sport chose the Tiger 100 model and when Irish farmer Ernie Lyons won the 1946 Manx Grand Prix on his private Triumph the factory began taking more of an interest.

In 1947 they gave a racing version its debut. Ridden by David Whitworth the bike had some success including a very good third place behind the works Norton of Artie Bell and the 'Saturno' Gilera of O. Clemencich at the Dutch TT.

In 1948 Triumph put its 'Grand Prix' model on the market having incorporated the ideas gleaned from the previous season's racing activities. Their idea was to make racing as accessible as possible by including as many production bike components as possible in the new machine.

The 500 cc twin was both light and fast. It weighed 314 lb compared with the 370 lb of the Manx Norton and the success of the over-the-counter racer persuaded the factory to enter a works team in racing again with such names as Bob Foster, Freddie Frith and Ken Bills.

Nine 'Grand Prix' Triumphs entered the 1948 TT and not one of them finished the race. After a spell back on the drawing board the designers rectified the faults

The 1948 'Grand Prix' Triumph racer. Both light and fast the idea was to include as many production components as possible ·

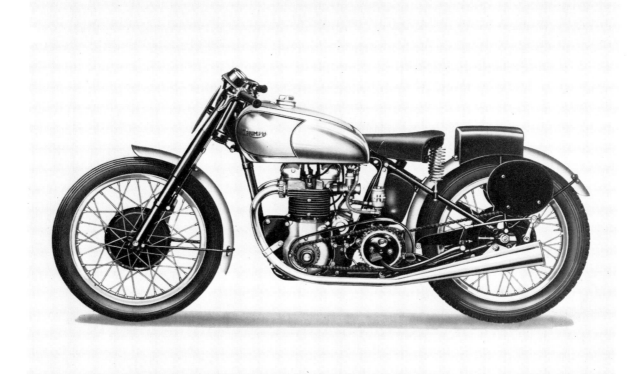

ABOVE LEFT *A 'Grand Prix' Triumph being wheeled to the line for the start of the 1953 Senior TT*

LEFT *A 'Grand Prix' Triumph and its proud owner pictured at the time of the 1954 Clubmans TT*

ABOVE *A 1957 Triumph being put through its paces at a Silverstone meeting*

The 'Grand Prix' Triumph in all its splendour. Its successes were restricted to the domestic scene

and there were some respectable results to show for their efforts before Triumph decided to pull out of racing.

Although no works team was in evidence during the following two years Triumph did continue to sell the 'Grand Prix' until the early 1950s.

We have to look to the late 50s before we see any further evidence of Triumph's success, this time in production racing which was to become their forte in later years.

In 1958 Dan Shorey and Mike Hailwood won the Thruton 500 miler on a twin carb Triumph Bonneville.

Velocette

Velocette's introduction to the 1950s cannot be described without mention of that legendary racing figure Freddie Frith who got the factory's involvement in world championship racing off to an immaculate start, winning every 350 grand prix in 1949.

It was during that innaugural year of the world championships that Velocette introduced new 350 and 500 cc models to their racing stables with double overhead cam engines and GP carburettors.

As in previous years the 350 Velo was the best bet for the factory riders. Frith won every 350 grand prix but on the 500 cc front the best results were a third in the Senior TT for Frith's team mate Ernie Lyons and a fifth at the Swiss Grand Prix for Frith.

All Velocette's successful 350 racers were descendants of the KTT, the factory's and indeed Britain's very first true production racer. It was derived from the KSS road machine and the first model produced featured several improvements. It was also a faster and more reliable machine than its single cylinder roadgoing sister.

For two decades the machines remained the same in basic concept but were obviously revised regularly in the fight against rival factories.

Like all other British factories their pre-war experiences were frustrated by the European manufacturer's commitment to supercharging and their efforts to combat this threat proved abortive.

During 1938 design chief Harold Willis, who first joined the factory eleven years earlier as a racer, and his crew built the 'Roarer' because of the advent of blown BMW, NSU, Gilera and AJS machines.

Although not as refined as some of the European examples Velocette were satisfied that the bike, a verti-

Paddock action from the 1940s which shows the racing thoroughbred which was to lay the foundation for Velocette's successes

cal twin with twin counter-rotating cranks, the left to drive the gearbox and the right to drive the supercharger, would act as an adequate holding operation.

However the death of Harold Willis was to prevent the machine ever having a competitive outing. Velocettes star rider Stanley Woods gave the bike a run in the practice of the last TT before the outbreak of War but the news of Willis's death put the project on ice.

Instead Woods used the existing single cylinder 500 machine but was on outclassed machinery finishing fourth. The singles were used for the rest of the year and quite expectedly, giving away so much horsepower the trend of Velocette being left behind continued until the end of the season.

Whether Velocette's fortunes would have altered had they perfected their blown twin will never really be known. All that is known is that in tests they managed

LEFT *Velocettes in battle in 1950 at the Belgian circuit of Floreffe. Reg Armstrong (Velocette) leads Bill Doran (AJS) and Frank Fry (Velocette)*

BELOW *A 1947 Mk VIII KTT racing Velocette. In 1949 Freddie Frith made a clean sweep of the 350 cc world champsionship on a similar machine*

to squeeze a very respectable 130 mph out of the prototype which weighed in at 370 lb.

After the War, with the clamp-down on super-charging, Velocettes results followed very much their pre-War pattern. The 350 was still the machine to beat as Frith's fantastic world championship win proved and the 500 single was always there.

The Birmingham factory's life in world championship racing during the 1950s was a limited one but they did turn the decade on a high note thanks to Freddie Frith's successor Bob Foster.

Frith had retired after his glorious 1949 season but that didn't mean the end of Velocette's chances in the 350 class. Foster captured the title again for his employers. He was world champion after wins in Belgium, Holland and Ireland and a second place at the Swiss Grand Prix.

Foster also had the distinction in 1950 of bettering Stanley Woods' Junior TT lap record which had stood since 1938 (though winner Artie Bell lapped even faster in 1950) but he was robbed of victory when the rear brake rod on his KTT broke. It was the same story in 1950 for the 500s. Their best result that year came from Reg Armstrong who finished sixth in the Senior TT.

The lack of results from the 500 after the War forced the factory to drop it for the 1951 season but added to

The Mk VIII KTT Velocette was the last in a long line of KTT racers from the factory. It was derived from the works model on which Stanley Woods won the Junior TT a decade before Freddie Frith's triumph

the stable that year was a 250 cc. This dohc model was basically a scaled down version of the all-conquering KTT and the three machines run by the factory were ridden by Bob Foster, Bill Lomas and Cecil Sandford.

Despite the resurgence in the lightweight class it was becoming obvious that Velocette's interest in racing was waning.

Results that year were not brilliant. Lomas and Foster took fifth and sixth respectively in the Junior TT. Other factory backed riders, Tommy Wood and Les Graham fared best at grand prix level. Wood won the Spanish Grand Prix with Graham second, and third and fourth places came at Spa for Bill Lomas and Cecil Sandford respectively.

At the Swiss Grand Prix, Graham was first home with Sandford second but these creditable performances on the KTT were not enough to secure the world title for Velocette a third year on the trot. That year it was to be Norton's turn thanks to the brilliance of rising star Geoff Duke.

Losing what had previously been a safe title seemed to further make up management's mind about scaling down Velocette's competition activities. Things were

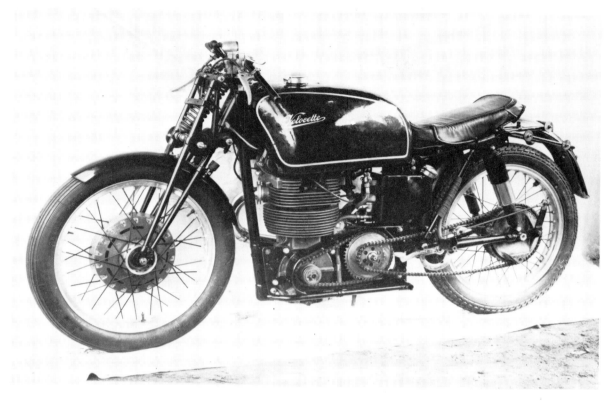

ABOVE *The 350 cc works racer as seen in 1952. The coming of the Italian factories was by this time shortening the life of the British racer*

RIGHT ABOVE *The Mk VIII KTT Velocette racer was built for speed. At £120 to the over-the-counter buyer it was virtually a replica of the machine used by the legendary Stanley Woods*

RIGHT BELOW *In those days the TT was a grand prix. Freddie Frith hurries his KTT on to victory in the 1949 Island races, part of his clean sweep*

lean on the 250 cc front in 1951 as well—naturally there were teething problems with the new machine.

Its best finishes were fifth places at the Isle of Man, and the Swiss, French and Ulster Grands Prix with a third at the Ulster.

At the end of 1951 it was announced that the 350 cc KTT was no longer to be produced. The glorious era was nearing its end. Further proof of this came in 1952 when Velocette made one more feeble effort at world championship racing with Les Graham and Cecil Sandford. Graham finished fourth in the 250 cc race at the Isle of Man on a machine which was down on speed and Graham had a few places in 350 grands prix.

While Velocette were winding down their operations in the 250 and 350 class they were secretly working on an in-line water cooled four cylinder machine with which to take on MV and Gilera.

Head of the project was long serving designer Percy Goodman but unfortunately he was taken ill and died after the preliminaries had been completed. A board meeting after his death determined that the project would be scrapped, the main reason being lack of funds to support the ambitious scheme.

In 1952 only 19 KTT Velos lined up for the Junior TT—a real sign of the times. From then on the marque slipped further and further out of competition save for the odd dabble in small time events.

In 1956 with the introduction of souped-up versions of the standard push rod models enticed some enthusiasts to choose Velocette for their sport including a crack at the 24 hour record at Montlhéry in France.

Vincent

The Stevenage factory's involvement in road racing like Velocette was restricted to the first half of the decade. Renowned more for its successes in the world of speed records the list of achievements in road racing circles is somewhat more limited than many of its fellow British manufacturers.

The story of post-War racing by Vincent began with the introduction of the improved series B Vincent Rapide after the frustrations of the 1930s with a 1000 cc V-twin, designed by Phil Irving which was prone to breaking gearboxes—such was the torque produced.

Irving had literally stumbled across the famous 47 degree V-twin design by juggling around drawings in 1936 and it was a re-designing of this initial lay-out which led to the machine which was to be used for countless speed records and racing appearances in the 1950s.

The sporting version of the series B Rapide was called the Black Shadow and this was followed by the

racing Black Lightning, taking their names from the black engine castings.

But the first racing version of the Rapide series appeared just before the outbreak of the Second World War at Donington Park ridden by Ginger Woods who set a new petrol-benzole lap record at the Midlands circuit.

Most of the big names to be associated with the factory actually worked at Stevenage. George Brown was on Vincent's books until 1951 when he left to set

RIGHT *George Brown on an HRD Vincent racer at the Brough airfield circuit in Yorkshire during the early 1950s*

RIGHT BELOW *An early Vincent racer on test. The racing models got their names from the famous black castings*

BELOW *Vincent mounted George Brown pictured at the 1950 TT. He was employed by the Stevenage factory until 1951 when he went his own way*

up his own motor cycle business, one of the most successful sidecar racers using a Vincent power-unit, Ted Davis also worked there and so too did John Surtees who had many of his early successes on the 500 cc single cylinder Grey Flash Vincent.

In 1952 the Vincent Black Shadow established eight new world records at Montlhéry near Paris ridden by Surtees, Ted Davis, Cyril Julian and Phil Heath among others. All production stopped in 1955.

But it was in that final year of production when Vincent set the new absolute world speed record through Russell Wright who set a new speed for the flying kilometre of 185 mph and Bobbie Burns established a new target for sidecar men of 163 mph!

Both records were set in New Zealand and were achieved on standard engines apart from racing cylinder heads and of course streamlining.

RIGHT *The best known Vincent rider of them all. George Brown on a 1000 cc Vincent Special at the Brighton Speed Trials in 1955, not a road race as such*

BELOW *Phil Heath on an HRD Vincent racer at Governors Bridge during the 1948 Clubmans TT*

2

The men -
the outstanding riders
of the decade

Ray Amm   Fergus Anderson   Reg Armstrong
George Brown   Keith Campbell   Harold Daniell
Geoff Duke   Freddie Frith   Bob Foster
Les Graham   Mike Hailwood   Werner Haas
Pip Harris   John Hartle   Bill Lomas
Sammy Miller   Derek Minter   Bob McIntyre
Eric Oliver   Tarquinio Provini   Tommy Robb
Cecil Sandford   Cyril Smith   John Surtees
Percy Tait   Luigi Taveri   Carlo Ubbiali

Ray Amm

Ray Amm was one of that very impressive wave of riders to emerge from Rhodesia but sadly his career was brought to a premature end during his first ride for MV at Imola in 1955. He was 29. Without doubt the lightly built Rhodesian was one of the brightest post-war riders to hit Europe, first arriving in Britain with his constant companion, his wife, Jill in 1951.

Riding his own two Nortons he quickly created an impression and soon attracted the attention of Norton race chief Joe Craig. A year later in 1952 he had secured himself a works contract with Norton and soon became the leader of the Norton team.

In 1953 he won both Junior and Senior TTs and was only the fifth rider ever to complete the Senior/Junior double at that time. In 1953 he had a classic duel with Gilera mounted Geoff Duke at the TT.

He won the 1953 Senior for Norton after pushing Duke so hard, with the help of a new record lap at 97.41 mph, that the British star fell at Quarter Bridge. It was in this race that another Briton riding for Italy, Les Graham on the MV, was killed on Bray Hill.

It was Graham's death which presented Amm with his opportunity to join the wealthier and better developed Italian factory, although it was not the first chance he'd had.

For some time he had withstood tempting offers from the Italians but his loyalty and remembering that start which Joe Craig had given him tied him to the British team.

A classic example of his brilliance and how the Italians desperately wanted to win him over was his 1954 TT performance in which he held off the might of the Italian challenge to head home Geoff Duke and his Gilera.

That year with machinery falling behind in terms of development he ended the season runner-up in both 350 and 500 cc world championships.

Before moving to the Gallarate factory at the beginning of 1955 had been involved in the experimental Norton 'kneeler' project and indeed was the only rider to give the bike a competitive outing at the North West 200 where he set a new 350 cc lap record before being forced to retire with teething problems.

Ray Amm pictured with fellow victor Rod Coleman in Sweden

Fergus Anderson

Twice 350 cc world champion, Fergus Anderson was one of that admirable breed of racers whose career spanned the pre and post war periods.

Anderson, a forthright journalist in addition to a world class motorcycle rider, became Scotland's first road racing world title holder. Many rushed to acclaim Jock Taylor the first Scottish world champion in 1980 but they forget about this exemplary gentleman who contributed 12 out of Moto Guzzi's 46 grand prix victories.

All his world championship successes came on the Italian factory's machinery and when at last he decided to retire from grand prix racing, after his second consecutive 350 cc championship in 1954, such was his loyalty to them that he became team manager.

Even when he had turned his back on the pressures of world championship racing he did not lose his touch. The year after his 'retirement' he won the 350 cc and 500 cc races at a Metter International in Belgium and along with his successors Bill Lomas and Dickie Dale he broke 350 cc world speed records at Montlhèry that same year.

He was 47 when he took Lomas and Dale under his wing on the Continental circus and had claimed to be the oldest TT victor four years earlier when at 43 he won the 250 cc race for Moto Guzzi.

Anderson's first world championship season for Moto Guzzi yielded only a best place of third in the 250 cc class at the 1949 Swiss Grand Prix and the following year a second at the Italian in the same class was all there was to shout about.

It was not until 1951 that he was to make his grand prix breakthrough and quite ironically it came on the 500 cc model from the factory which had such a chequered career and which was not to figure in any of Anderson's title successes.

After a fourth place in the French Grand Prix at 250 cc level, Anderson won the 500 cc Swiss Grand Prix that same year, heading home Reg Armstrong on the AJS. This was one of two 500 cc grand prix victories he was to score for the factory, the other coming at the Spanish Grand Prix in 1953.

In 1952 the first of a long succession of grand prix

Scotland's first world champion, Fergus Anderson

victories came for Anderson on the smaller singles. He won the 250 cc race in Switzerland and the lightweight TT and so enthusiastic about the bike's performance was he that he eventually persuaded designer Giulio Carcano to produce a 350 cc version of the world-beater which was to lead to his two world titles.

First victory for the 350 cc machine came at the 1953 Dutch TT in the hands of Enrico Lorenzetti, where Anderson crossed the line second in the 250 cc race. At the Ulster Grand Prix he finished third in the 250 cc race and began to find some 350 cc form at the Italian Grand Prix where he crossed the line behind victor Lorenzetti.

In Spain he finished third but then never looked back as he scored successive victories in Switzerland and Belgium and third in the Isle of Man on his way to he first world crown.

Victories in Holland, Italy, Spain and Switzerland paved the way for his glorious retirement from grand prix racing in 1954 which, in conjunction with a second in Belgium, was enough to retain his title ahead of Ray Amm of Rhodesia on a Norton.

Reg Armstrong

Though he never became a world champion during his career, which ended midway through the 1950s, Ireland's Reg Armstrong is the country's second most successful world championship campaigner in world championship history.

Perhaps a 'nearly man' tag is appropriate for this star who was one of the most consistent riders of the period acting as a brilliant support rider for a number of colleagues.

Apart from Ralph Bryans, who shone in the following decade with 11 grand prix victories, Armstrong achieved more than any other Irish representative.

In all he scored seven grand prix victories in a career in which he served six different factories— Gilera, his most successful link, Norton, Velocette, NSU, Moto Guzzi and AJS.

On three occasions, 1952 (Norton) 1953 and 1955 (Gilera) he finished runner-up to team mate Geoff Duke in world title chases. On the earliest occasion both he and Duke were riding for Joe Craig's Norton squad but then both had later succumbed to the pressure of Italian race chiefs.

His earliest world championship efforts came on AJS 7R machinery only a year after the 'boy racer' had started to roll off the production line. And in that innaugural 1949 world championship season his best result came on his home ground in the Ulster Grand Prix with third spot.

This was the year, or course, when Grimsby's Freddie Frith made a clean sweep of the 350 cc competition for the rival Velocette factory. Armstrong's year had been a good one for in addition to third in Ireland he finished fourth in Switzerland, fifth at the TT and sixth at the Belgian Grand Prix.

His riding ability had been such that he split the works Velocettes of Frith and Bob Foster, finishing runner-up in the 350 cc title chase.

Bearing in mind Frith's runaway victory in 1949 and subsequent retirement it wasn't too surprising to see Armstrong's name linked with Velocette for the 1950 battle.

But the switch was to hold little success for Armstrong whose best placing, before a return to AJS for 1951, again came on his home ground with a second.

Back on AJS there was still no joy to come for Armstrong. His best outing of the year came at the Swiss Grand Prix where he finished second and third on 500 cc and 350 cc machines respectively.

Out of the top three in the final reckoning he joined Norton for the following season and here began his successful partnership with Geoff Duke.

This was to be his finest season. In addition to winning the Senior TT for Norton, highlighted by that famous chain snapping incident which happened just seconds after he crossed the finishing line, he completed a 350 and 500 cc double for the factory at the German Grand Prix. Reward for his efforts were a second spot behind Duke in the 350 cc title and third behind Umberto Masetti (Gilera) and Les Graham (MV Agusta) in the 500 cc class.

By 1953 Armstrong had joined the Italian Gilera factory and was backing up his 500 cc rides with 125 cc and 250 cc appearances for NSU. It was with NSU that he scored his only grand prix victory of the year, again at home. But this was to be a very historic victory for he was the first 250 cc class winner on the new Dundrod Ulster Grand Prix circuit.

Earlier in the year he had been campaigning at 250 cc level for the Italian Moto Guzzi factory with fellow countryman Fergus Anderson and Enrico Lorenzetti and finished third at the Dutch TT but by the time his home event had arrived NSU had secured his services alongside German star Werner Haas.

Those were busy days for Armstrong for in addition

Reg Armstrong and the 500 Gilera in 1955. He remains one of Ireland's most successful grand prix riders

to riding 250 cc machines for the Germans he also found himself in the saddle of a 125 cc racer on which he scored a best 1953 placing of third at the Ulster.

But his exploits on the smaller machines did not bring a top three position at the end of the year. For this he had to rely again on his trusty 500 cc Gilera alongside Duke behind whom he finished again in the runner-up spot.

During the final three years of his career all his major achievements were restricted to the 'blue riband' class and for Gilera.

Again in 1955 he backed-up Duke superbly around Europe with the runners-up spot enhanced by a Spanish Grand Prix victory. The only win of his final year of world championship action came at the German Grand Prix.

George Brown

George Brown, who died in 1979 at the age of 67, was chief tester at the Stevenage-based Vincent works and was a successful road racer before turning to sprinting in which he set numerous world records on his famous 998 cc and 1147 cc *Nero* and *Super Nero* Vincent machines.

George, who later left Vincent to establish his own motor cycle business in Stevenage, joined Vincent in 1934 and it is said that his loyalty to the company deprived him of a Norton works ride in the early 1950s.

He retired from road racing after Les Graham's death during the 1953 TT. His mind was further made up to leave the track when he himself crashed soon afterwards at Cadwell Park and Eppynt.

From then his efforts were concentrated on speed records. He sprinted until 1967 at international level but then reached the FIM's upper age limit for international competition of 55 and channelled his efforts into national events.

Keith Campbell

Keith Campbell will always be remembered as the first Australian rider to win a world championship, which he did for Moto Guzzi in the 350 cc title chase of 1957.

That year he held off Gilera works rider Bob McIntyre and Libero Liberati to lift the crown but alas, after a long struggle to establish himself in Europe that Italians chose to withdraw from grand prix racing at the end of that same year.

Like so many Australians who were to follow in Campbell's footsteps, he sacrificed everything, including engineering studies against his parents wishes, to get to Europe.

His first appearance in Europe was at the Manx Grand Prix in 1951 but what happened to him would normally have been enough to send a rider packing with his tail between his legs. He crashed after working his way up to third place on his 350 Velocette and that was to be the first frustrating step in eight years of climbing to the top.

After biting the dust at the Verandah he returned home to win the 350 cc South Australian Championship on his special Velocette. He used to make his own cams for the machine using a bench grinder!

Not deterred by what had happened on his first visit to Europe the hard-riding Melbourne rider was back the following year with his 10/10ths riding style for which he was to become renowned.

That year he finished sixth in the Manx and with no money to go home he started working for Nortons. It was while working there that he met up with Gordon Laing, whom he was to partner on several Continental outings.

Still the winning sequence he had been looking for eluded him but despite the lack of success he managed to arm himself with two short-stroke Nortons for the 1954 season. During this season frustration was to plague him once again.

He crashed during practice for the TT and so desperate was he to start winning that he rode at the Belgian Grand Prix with a plaster cast on his left hand, working wonders to finish fifth with his handicap.

After a double win at Vesoul later that year he returned to Australia where he again captured the 350 cc class at the South Australian championships.

With determination like Campbell's it was only a matter of time before everything clicked into place and that happened during 1955. Steadily his European form improved and by the end of the 1956 season the works teams were showing a real interest in the rough diamond from down under.

At Senigallia he was loaned a 350 Moto Guzzi by the factory to help their chances. His brief was to make things look good for the first half dozen laps and then

allow team mates Ken Kavanagh and Dickie Dale take the honours.

But the factory had underestimated Campbell's desperation. He had been grovelling around Europe for six long years waiting for his big break and there was no chance of him obeying their orders.

Needless to say Campbell won the race and half expected to be black-listed by the Italians.

The rest is history. Everything fell into place in his seventh season in Europe. He repaid Moto Guzzi for their faith in him (they didn't turn their back on him after his disobedience) and won the 1957 world crown by eight points from Bob McIntyre and Italian Libero Liberati both on Gileras.

But what a tragedy that the mass exit by the Italian factories was to happen in that same season. It had taken Campbell seven long years to achieve his finest hour and then it was all over.

In 1958 Campbell rode private Nortons and was fatally injured in a crash in France.

Harold Daniell

Although not one of the most prolific riders throughout the whole of the decade Harold Daniell brought in the 1950s in style.

He was the originator of the term 'featherbed' for the new Nortons introduced at the turn of the decade. The term stuck after his initial description following test rides. He was then Norton's team leader and by the time the 1950s had arrived had won three TTs.

Daniell was an unmistakeable figure in any paddock. A friendly jovial character, plump and bespectacled. Born in London he began his racing career at circuits like Brooklands and Donington Park and his big break-through came in 1933 when he won the Senior Manx Grand Prix.

His reward was a works ride with AJS but he felt more at home on the superbly tuned Norton Steve Lancefield prepared for him. By 1938 he was a Norton works rider and he justified his machinery by winning the Senior TT from Stanley Woods, setting a new lap record of 91 mph—the first sub 25 minute lap.

His record stood for an amazing 12 years, such was the calibre of the man—though, of course, the war was partly responsible. He died at the age of 57 in 1967, having retired from racing in 1951.

A friendly, jovial character, plump and bespectacled Harold Daniell was a welcome sight in any paddock. He retired from racing in 1951 after a distinguished career with Norton

95

Geoff Duke

If we were to talk about an award for the rider of the decade then surely this man, Geoff Duke, would have a very strong claim to that title.

One of the most prolific riders ever to be produced in Britain, Duke's name stands out head and shoulders above most other exponents of this period. During his 1950s heyday he captured six world titles, three for Norton and three for the Italian Gilera factory after finally giving in to pressure to join them.

He was a great ambassador figure and many believe him to have been the first of the modern racers with such innovations as one piece leathers. He was one of the first riders to create interest in other quarters by receiving the OBE for his outstanding achievements in motor cycle sport. At the time of his visit to Buckingham Palace only one other rider, Freddie Frith, had been decorated in 1950.

Ironically it was not as a road racer that Geoff Duke began the road to stardom. After being demobbed in 1947, having had an interest in motor cycles since his teenage days, he joined BSA in the trials workshops. At that time he owned his own 350 BSA and was soon representing his company in team trial events.

Quite amazingly Duke never took part in a road race until he was 26 years old. In modern times it's doubtful whether any enthusiast could leave his entry to the sport that late and still hope to make a name for himself . . . but Duke was no ordinary rider.

He was persuaded to swing his leg over a Norton road racer by Irish star Artie Bell and his debut came in the 1948 Senior Manx Grand Prix. The talent was there right from the start . . . he led before a split tank put him out of the running!

The following year he won the Senior Clubmans race on the Island, won the Senior Manx Grand Prix and finished second in the Junior event. It was inevitable that Duke's talents would be spotted by the works teams and Norton were the lucky outfit to get his signature.

One of the greatest riders of all time, Geoff Duke's career started as a works trials rider

He won just about every race he entered and perhaps his most impressive performance during those early years of his career was winning the Senior TT at his first attempt. He carried out his task at a record speed of 92.27 with a record lap of 93.33 and was second in the Junior event that same year.

Taking Duke's achievement in terms of competition today it would be virtually impossible to repeat his amazing feat. But what has to be remembered is that the Manx Grand Prix in the 1950s was much more akin to TT racing than it is today. The whole standard of competition has a greater differential today.

In 1951 he returned victorious to the Isle of Man in both Junior and Senior events and to cap a brilliant year for the British factory he won both 350 and 500 cc world championships. He was the first rider ever to hold both titles in one year.

But Duke's golden days with Norton were coming to an end thanks to the advent of the Italian multis and in 1952 he could not repeat the sensation of the previous season. He regained the 350 world crown but Umberto Masetti beat him to the post in the blue riband class on his superior Gilera.

Such was his loyalty to Norton that it was to drive him out of the sport momentarily. Kept at bay by the powerful Italian factories during 1952 Duke switched to car racing in 1953 out of frustration, racing an Aston Martin DB2 with considerably less success than his two-wheeled efforts.

He could stand the temptation no longer and accepted an offer from Gilera to come back into racing later that year. Then began the second part of a brilliant career.

What a glorious return to road racing! He was 500 cc world champion for the Italians from 1953 to 1955.

Then of course in 1956 came the episode which was to be retold time and time again when his career was to be discussed or written about. After supporting fellow grand prix riders in a start money strike at the 1955 Dutch TT, Duke was singled out as one of the ring leaders and suspended by the FIM for the first half of the 1956 season.

His chances of a title that year were ruined by this action. His 500 cc world championship win of 1955 was to be his last.

Another contributing factor to his decline was the emergence of another brilliant Briton . . . John Surtees, who by this time had joined Gilera's arch rivals MV and who was stringing results together at a prolific rate.

So no joy for Duke in 1956 and it was to be the same in 1957 with a crash at Imola early in the year putting him out of action for four races. When Gilera pulled out of racing at the end of 1957 it was virtually the end of the road for Duke.

In 1958 he rode a BMW with limited success and in 1959 he was back on a Norton again but there could be no repeat of the form which had made him the most rated man of the mid-Fifties.

After 1959 he tried car racing again but once again it was a short-lived occupation. After a crash in Sweden in 1961 he announced his retirement.

Bob Foster

Gloucestershire's Bob Foster was one of those amazing riders whose career spanned both pre and postwar periods. He won his first TT back in 1936 and then became 350 cc world champion 14 years later!

Much of his pre-war activities were shared between road racing and trials riding at which he achieved expert status and was very rarely missing from the country's leading trials events. Of the three seasons immediately prior to World War Two were spent riding AJS machines and much of that time in a development role. In the 1938 Senior TT he rode AJS's air-cooled four cylinder which ironically gave up the ghost through overheating problems and then he was involved in the testing of the watercooled version of the four.

After initial tests at Brooklands and Donington Park Foster gave the bike three competitive outings. Once at the North West 200 where it blew a cylinder head gasket when he was leading, once in the Senior TT when he crossed the line 13th and once at the Ulster Grand Prix where fouled plugs put and end to his race. Things were a little better for AJS team mate Walter Rusk. He got home 11th in the Senior TT and set the first 100 mph lap of the Ulster Grand Prix, when it was on the Clady course on the V4 before having to retire.

Foster's lead in to the 1950s and that glorious opening year of the decade for him started back in 1948 when the legendary Stanley Woods persuaded him to accompany him to Moto Guzzi's Mandello factory in Italy to test ride their 1949 offerings.

The visit led to Foster splitting his loyalties between the Italians, who had been impressed by Foster's world championship form, particularly his 1947 Junior TT win for Velocette, and AJS.

That was at 500 cc level but he stuck with Velocette for his 350 cc exploits preferring the reliability of the

KTT. What a wise move it was for it was on a Velocette that he was to lift that covetted crown just a year later.

The Guzzi during 1949 proved troublesome. He rode it three times. The first outing came at the Isle of Man where the most frustrating moment of his career happened. He was leading the Senior event on the final lap when the primary drive broke on Sulby Straight forcing him out of contention. If he had won that event he would have scored victories in Lightweight, Junior and Senior events during his life as a racer. The other Guzzi rides came at Spa and at the Ulster Grand Prix where he retired both times.

But the frustrations of 1949 were to be remedied the following season when Foster took over from Freddie Frith as number one Velocette rider in the 350 cc world championship chase. Frith had retired on a brilliant note winning every grand prix in the inaugural 350 series—it was a tall order for anyone to try and emulate that sort of form. He didn't win every round in 1950 but wins at the Belgian and Ulster grands prix were enough to give him the title.

After winning the 1950 350 cc world championship Foster was set to retire but Velocette persuaded him to stay on another year and add his valuable experience to a three man team comprising Cecil Sandford and Bill Lomas in addition to himself.

Velocette were to contest the 250 cc world championship the following year and although both 250 and 350 machines turned out to be no match for the Italian Moto Guzzis and Benellis at the end of the day Foster stuck to his brief in his accepted professional manner.

Bob Foster and an early Moto Guzzi with which he was associated

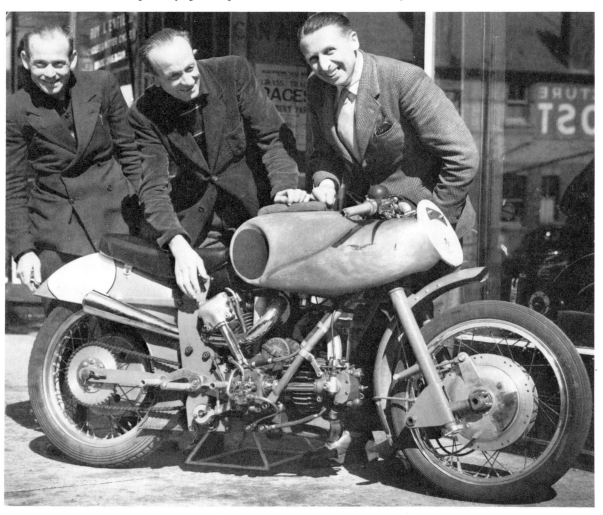

Freddie Frith

Although he never actually raced in the 1950s, having retired at the end of the first year of the world championships it is important to include, in our look back at the decade, the name of Freddie Frith. This is simply because he is one of the great legends of our sport.

Early writers refer to Grimsby's most famous motor cycling son with such adjectives as 'chivalrous' and 'honourable' . . . 'the Galahad in leathers'.

Adjectives apart he was the greatest 350 cc rider of that first year of world championship competition as his clean sweep of the grand prix calendar proved. That was to be his only world crown but because of its dating it is so often referred to by historians.

With motor cycle competition already in his family in the form of an enthusiastic father, Freddie was soon on the road to stardom. He graduated from Grimsby area grasstracks on a BSA 250 to the 1930 Manx Grand Prix his first of many visits to the Isle of Man on a KTT Velocette.

His TT record was prolific. He was the first to win a Junior TT at over 80 mph in 1936 and the following year he set the first 90 mph plus lap of the Island. He never failed to gain a place in any TT he finished and those numbered nine out of 12 starts.

During 1949 he won the Junior TT and the grands prix in Switzerland, Holland, Belgium and Ulster without dropping a single point. It was a tall order for anyone during the 1950s to repeat.

His pre-war successes came on Norton machinery and then when peace returned he used Velocettes until his retirement.

Grimsby's most famous motorcycling son, Freddie Frith. 'Chivalrous' and 'honourable' they called him

Les Graham

Tragically the career of this highly respected rider was brought to an end with a crash on Bray Hill in the 1953 Senior TT after he had just given the MV factory their big breakthrough in the Isle of Man. Graham, who first rode for MV in 1951 after serving with AJS, for whom he won the first 500 cc world title in 1949, had just won the 125 cc TT for the Italian factory when fate struck.

He was one of the leading British riders in both pre and post war periods. During the War he served as a bomber pilot and was awarded the DFC for his efforts.

When peace returned he led the AJS team and his 1949 500 cc world championship triumph was to be the British team's only success in the classics. His victorious year came on the 'Porcupine' twin and in that same year he was leading the Senior TT when mechanical failure robbed him of victory.

Graham's association with MV was a very deep one. He was not simply a rider but someone to whom the Gallarate team owe a great deal in the story of the development of their machines.

True, in later years MV were to reach almost

perfection, but it was under the brilliance of Graham that they were able to sort out the scores of initial problems they had.

When Graham first rode the four cylinder machines they were fast, unreliable and didn't handle. But by the time 1953 had arrived Graham had almost got the machines to a respectable race order.

Les Graham in the Isle of Man in 1952. Before his death in 1953 he had set MV on the road to success

Werner Haas

West German star Werner Haas became 125 cc and 250 cc world champion in 1953 and the feat of becoming a double world champion has only been repeated by one other German rider, Anton Mang.

When referring to Haas's brilliant career it must always be regarded as 'what might have been' for although he was world champion on three occasions, twice in 1953 and once in 1954 (250 cc), this was only the tip of the iceberg. His potential was as exciting as the greatest of riders in this period.

Haas's world championship career was linked exclusively to the NSU factory and when they withdrew from grand prix competition in 1954 he decided to retire.

This was only two years after his first ride for the factory and was obviously far too premature!

In his first appearance for NSU in his home grand prix Haas shocked the all conquering Italian Mondial and Guzzi factories in the 125 and 250 classes. The following season, after that sensational debut, the combination of Haas and NSU reigned supreme winning both 125 and 250 world titles.

Haas had the same sort of effect on the opposition when he and NSU arrived at the Isle of Man TT races. In 1953 he finished second in the 125 and 250 classes. The following year he retired in the 125 race but won the 250 event with a fastest lap of 91.22 mph.

Although NSU's racing activities died on a works basis at the end of 1954 Haas lived on but out of the limelight until he was killed in an air crash in 1956.

Werner Haas. Many feel his career never reached its peak. He decided to retire at the same time as his employers, NSU

Mike Hailwood

Although mainly associated with the 1960s Mike Hailwood's career did begin during the previous decade, when in 1957 he made his racing debut on a 125 cc MV.

That historic ride came at Oulton Park when he was just 17 years old and he shouldn't even have been there! He should have been completing the Scottish Six Days on a Triumph Tiger Cub. But his boredom in the Scottish Highlands drove him south to Cheshire where he finished in a midfield position after a mediocre start.

Stanley Michael Bailey's first taste of speed had come on the Oxford by-pass, the city of spires being his birthplace. He had at that time a BSA Gold Star and with no speed limits in those days he squeezed a frightening 112 mph out of his mount on the open road. Like many road racers Mike lied about his age to get into international competition. Still 17 he put his age up to 18 and then baffled everybody by staying 21 for two years!

His first win during his opening year of competition came at Blandford Camp in Dorset on a 200 cc MV Modello Sport. After that initial year's racing Mike went to South Africa to gain experience and on his return he had his first look at the Isle of Man which was to be the stage of many a glorious moment later in his career. There was little to shout about on his first TT appearance as an 18 year old. He finished seventh, twelfth, thirteenth and third in his four starts.

By the end of the decade Mike Hailwood (centre) had won his first world championship race. He is pictured with Ernst Degner (left) and Gary Hocking

That same year he won three out of the four ACU Star meetings which were the forerunners of the British championship series.

With his father the head of the massive Kings of Oxford motor cycle network Mike had few financial worries which hinder the progress of many of today's rising stars. But that made little difference to the progress being made by the man who was to go on to become the greatest motor cycle racer of all time in many people's minds.

His world championship breakthrough came in Northern Ireland when in 1959 he won the 125 cc Ulster Grand Prix on a Ducati.

Pip Harris

Peter Valentine Harris, known to everyone as 'Pip' Harris was one of Britain's best known sidecar racing ambassadors of the 1950s, his career coming to an end early in the 1960s.

Like many of those early sidecar heroes his career began on the grass and he got in to road racing by way of a merger of the two sports between 1948 and 1949, after which he realised that there was no way he could be successful with split loyalties and so with the world championships underway he turned full time sidecar road racer.

During his first years on the track he used the almost universally accepted British engines to power his outfits but in 1959 with the amazing BMW reign already started he switched to the German marque.

His best world championship placings came in 1956 and 1960 when he finished third both times. In 1956 he used a Norton outfit to finish behind Willie Noll of West Germany and Fritz Hillebrand another German, both of whom used BMWs. Harris also used a Matchless power unit during this period but with less success.

His 1960 achievement, this time on a BMW powered outfit he ended the world championship season behind Germany's legendary Helmut Fath and the Swiss Fritz Scheidegger. Both of course were BMW users.

Harris's TT record was a very respectable one. During the 1950s he entered every TT from 1954 onwards and never finished below fourth spot. He did however have a few breakdowns. His best finish came in 1956 when he was second to Hillebrand on a Norton, repeating the same feat in 1960 behind Fath on a BMW.

His other best results came in 1955 on a Matchless and 1961 on a BMW when he finished third each time.

Pip Harris near the end of his most respectable career

John Hartle

John Hartle's career began in 1954 and spanned both that decade and the one which followed becoming one of the most prominent British riders of his day.

Born in Chapel-en-le-Frith Hartle's international racing career began at Olivers Mount, Scarborough and it was a tragic irony that this Yorkshire circuit was to see his last ever ride in 1968 following a crash on the steep climb from the Mere Hairpin.

But the 50s for Hartle were golden days and some of his finest achievements came during this period. With talent like his it came as no surprise when Norton offered him a works ride soon after his debut ride and thereafter began a period of great success, which quite inevitably was to culminate in the Italian super-powers offering him a contract.

After Manx Grand Prix experience, he first rode in the TT in 1955 on a Norton and recorded the modest achievements of a sixth in the Junior and 13th in the Senior races. It was in the same year that John Surtees was picked up by Norton. Surtees meanwhile was

showing the sort of form which was eventually to take him to world championships on both motor cycles and in cars and was only with Norton for a season with Hartle before moving on to MV.

But that was not to be the end of Hartle's partnership days with Surtees. In 1957 Hartle was signed up by the Italians and was back alongside his former team mate.

Although he did not win a TT during the 1950s he rode with great distinction around the Mountain circuit. Bob McIntyre had become the first man to lap the TT course at over 100 mph in 1957 on a Gilera and Hartle had the somewhat lesser distinction of being the second man to equal that feat on an MV a year later.

The nearest Hartle came to winning a TT during our chosen period was in 1959 when he finished runner up to Surtees in the 1959 Junior. He was of course to record his only TT triumph the following season for MV when he won the Junior.

John Hartle—'the nearly man'

Bill Lomas

How many of today's racers would have the willpower to retire from the game at 29 years of age? Well that's exactly what Bill Lomas did when Moto Guzzi decided to pull out of racing in 1957.

Moto Guzzi were the last in a line of factories for whom Lomas rode and it was an obvious desire not to drop his standards of machinery which persuaded him to end his career at a somewhat early age.

His first signs of promise emerged in post-war racing at Lincolnshire's Cadwell Park. He was the circuits champion at 250, 350 and 500 cc level from 1948 to 1950 having scuttled the opposition of the day with a JAP powered Royal Enfield rolling chassis.

Lomas was a versatile motor cyclist and exuded style and competence in every field of the sport he turned to. A fine example of his prowess in other areas were his days with the James trials team for whom he finished fourth in the Scottish Six Days Trial and third in the British Experts Trial before becoming completely wrapped up in road racing.

Bob Foster was his first team mate in the Velocette line-up with whom he stayed for two seasons before the changing of contracts to AJS, NSU, MV and Moto Guzzi, began.

His move to Moto Guzzi must go down as one of the most unusual transfers in the history of road racing.

At that time he was riding for MV and for the 1955 TT he was due to represent the Italian factory at 125 and 250 level and AJS in the bigger classes on their 350 and 500 machines.

But AJS were not having any of that. They insisted that he solely represent them or else they would withdraw from the TT races. Being known as a straight outspoken character Lomas stuck to his guns and forced AJS to save face and pull out of the 1955 TT series.

Keeping their ears to the ground were Moto Guzzi who obviously wanted the best men on their machines and when team manager and former racer Fergus Anderson stepped forward to offer Lomas the use of his company's machines there started Lomas's two year association with the factory.

Lomas repaid Guzzi's faith in him by winning the Junior event but couldn't quite match this performance at Senior level with a seventh place.

He also performed well for his other Italian employers winning the 250 race and finishing fourth in the 125 race for MV.

It was obvious that his success for Moto Guzzi would keep him under their wing. That same season Lomas won them the 350 cc world championship and in 1956 he retained the title. With Moto Guzzi joining forces with Mondial and Gilera in the mass withdrawal from the sport in 1957 so too went Lomas.

Bob McIntyre

June 6, 1957 will always be remembered as the greatest day in the career of Bob McIntyre. It was the day in which he became the first rider to lap the Isle of Man TT course at over 100 mph!

Despite this marvellous achievement which still counts for more today than most other TT achievements Robert McGregor McIntyre the popular Glaswegian was never to win a world championship before his untimely death, aged 33, riding an ex-perimental five-speed Norton at Oulton Park in 1962.

McIntyre lapped at 101.12 mph on his way to Senior victory for Gilera the factory whose team he was leading in 1957. The closest anyone had come to that before was 99.97 mph recorded by Geoff Duke, also on a Gilera, two years before.

He was held by almost everyone at the time to be the greatest rider never to win a world championship. He came frustratingly close to a world title in 1957 when all he had to do was go out and win the Italian Grand Prix at Monza on his Gilera, which was an achievement well within his capabilities, but on the eve of the race he was taken ill and did not recover in time to make the grid.

Bob 'Mac' began racing on a 500 cc Norton, a real cut price racer, back in 1951 but then drifted away from the roads by taking up scrambling. When he did return his first serious race came at Beveridge Park, Kirkaldy, where he raced a borrowed 350 cc BSA.

The first of those glorious Isle of Man appearances was to come in 1952 when, after winning the Junior Manx Grand Prix, he finished runner up in the Senior event, quite incredibly on the same machine.

McIntyre's list of achievements is littered with TT highspots. In addition to his memorable double of 1957 he was second in the 1955 Junior on a Norton and then in 1959 chased John Surtees and the mighty MV around the Mountain circuit on his production Norton and AJS machinery before retirement put him out of the Junior and clutch trouble dropped him to fifth place in the Senior.

It was in his role as an underdog, with standard machinery, that McIntyre always seemed to be more at home. Despite a glorious season in 1957 for Gilera it was observed that he was always at his keenest on the private mounts. In between his factory stints during the 50s which took him to AJS and Gilera he is best remembered for his long association with Scottish tuner Joe Potts.

At the start of the 60s McIntyre was loaned works Honda machinery and became a factory runner for the 1962 season. It was during this year that he again came close to a world crown finishing runner-up in the 250 class but alas his year was to end on such a tragic note with his Oulton Park accident.

Sammy Miller

When a person reaches the top of the tree in two fields of a sport then that achievement speaks volumes. Such is the case of world famous trials rider Sammy Miller, now retired from top class competition, but who more than held his own as a world championship road racer before he joined the 'feet-up' game.

Born in 1935, Irishman Sammy was a member of the Italian works Mondial team in 1956 and 1957. As well as acting as a perfect ambassador in Irish road racing events he campaigned on a world championship basis and finished third in the 1957 250 cc championship behind team mates Cecil Sandford and Tarquinio Provini.

A TT lover Sammy rode four different types of machinery during his Isle of Man exploits from 1956–1958. He represented Mondial, Ducati, NSU and CZ in the 125 and 250 classes during these years.

His best placings were in 1957 and 1958 when he

finished fourth in the 125 event on Mondial and Ducatis respectively.

In 1958 Sammy took the decision to turn his back on road racing and begin his legendary rise to fame in the trials world. However he still maintains an avid interest in road racing and visits the TT races regularly.

His proudest possession at his own museum is a fully restored AJS V4 like the one which Walter Rusk used to produce the first 100 mph lap of the Clady circuit, scene of the Ulster Grand Prix until the early 1950s.

Derek Minter

Derek Minter was one of Britain's leading riders during the late 1950s and the 1960s. His story begins at Brands Hatch where he made his first appearance on a 500 cc BSA Gold Star and from then on his progress never stopped. His name is always linked first to Brands Hatch because of the proximity of his home town of Canterbury where he was born in 1932.

His formative years as a road racer, his interest in motor cycle sport having started during his national service years with trials riding, were spent on 350 and 500 cc Norton machines. His career really began to take off in 1958 when he took the decision to turn full time professional and venture abroad for the first time with his Nortons. He rode a variety of machinery during his apprenticeship years and was one of the long-established Cotton factory's best ever runners.

He met with a fair amount of success during his first ambitious seasons, finishing third and fourth at the Dutch TT and fourth at the Belgian Grand Prix but what really put his name into everybody's mind was the day he beat 500 cc world champion John Surtees on the MV at Brands Hatch in 1958.

His confidence grew as the decade got older. The 1950s had served as a great foundation for *The Mint* and the best was to come in the 1960s!

'The Mint' scratching on a 250 cc REG at Brands Hatch in 1957

Eric Oliver

Eric Oliver was Britain's most successful ever sidecar driver with four world titles to his credit when he died in hospital near his Windsor home at the beginning of 1980 following a heart attack.

He was the very first world sidecar champion winning the innaugural 1949 series and was champion again in 1950, 1951, and 1953. He had been the only British world sidecar champion along with Cyril Smith (1952) when George O'Dell finally put Britain's name back on the roll of honour in 1978.

Eric had been interested in solo racing in his pre-war day but in the late 40s he began concentrating solely on sidecar racing with great effect.

Credited with the introduction of the 'kneeler' type of outfit used universally today, Oliver's loyalty to the British Norton power unit contributed greatly to his downfall with the advent of the all-conquering BMW engine.

It was West German Willie Noll who took the crown from him in 1954 marking the first of many world championships for the Germans.

During his world championship career which lasted six years Eric won 18 grands prix and one of these was the historic sidecar TT of 1954 which was the first to be held in the Island (on the Clypse circuit) since 1925! The BMW onslaught had already started at that time but Oliver's skill saw him through for victory against Fritz Hillebrand and Willie Noll.

In addition to his riding skills Oliver's chances were always enhanced by the thorough preparation of his Norton Watsonian outfit, all carried out by himself.

An extremely dedicated character his place in history is perhaps best put into perspective by comparing his achievements with today's British sidecar heroes like Jock Taylor.

Jock was the toast of Britain when he won the 1980 world sidecar championship. He became *Motor Cycle News* Man of the Year . . . but he still needs another three world crowns to equal Oliver's outstanding achievement!

Eric Oliver in the Isle of Man. It was 25 years before George O'Dell gave Britain another world champion

Tarquinio Provini

Tarquinio Provini was one of those intelligent easy to work with, riders whom all designers and mechanics dream about. Employed by both MV and Mondial, Provini was renowned for a quality which enabled him to get the very best out of a machine and this quality bore fruit in 1957, when he became 125 cc world champion for Mondial and in 1958 when he clinched the 250 cc title for MV.

Like many of his fellow countrymen whose careers began in the 1950s his achievements spanned both this decade and the 1960s. His first Isle of Man appearance came in 1955 and after a two year apprenticeship he won the 125 race in 1957 which was to help him on his way to the world title. The following year his 250 cc world championship came after a win in the corresponding class in the Isle of Man series.

Ironically in 1959 a glorious double at the Isle of Man in 125 and 250 classes for MV was to leave him short on points in both world championship series. In the 125 class he finished the season runner-up to team mate Carlo Ubbiali and suffered the same fate in the 250 class again behind his hard-riding partner.

Although Provini was offered contracts which would have taken him into the blue riband 500 cc class he resisted them all to concentrate on the less publicised smaller classes.

Tommy Robb

Ulsterman Tommy Robb's career began in 1955 after trying his hand at trials and scrambles. Like so many men destined for stardom it was only a short time before the talent spotters had him in their sights.

At this time he was campaigning in the 200 cc class in his country's national championships over the notorious road circuits which still exist today.

Assistance came along in a very short time and he furthered his career on a 175 MV, moving to greater things in 1957 when he joined Geoff Monty's team which was to bring with it the opportunity to ride AJS, Matchless, Norton and Ducati machinery.

Quite incredibly Robb's career was to take place over three decades but his first taste of grand prix racing came at the end of the 50s when he rode a 250 MZ in selected grands prix. One of his best early results came at Monza where he finished sixth in the Italian Grand Prix on the MZ.

Cecil Sandford

The story of Cecil Sandford's distinguished career is one of 'firsts'. In 1952 he became the first British rider to win a 125 cc world title and then five years later he completed a prestigious double by becoming the first Briton to win the 250 world championship.

There was double joy for him in 1952 for his 125 world title marked a breakthrough in his class for his employers at that time, MV, who had had to play second fiddle to Mondial during the first three years of the world championships.

After a baptism in grass tracking he made the transition to road racing after two years and within three years was a world champion. His second world title came for Mondial and quite incredibly he again forged a breakthrough for an Italian factory for this was the first title in this class that Mondial had lifted.

With wins at the TT and Ulster Grands Prix he secured his 250 cc crown and having achieved these heights he chose to call it a day retiring as 250 world champion. How many riders would have that sort of strength of character today?

In addition to MV and Mondial, Sandford rode AJS, Moto Guzzi, Velocette and DKW machinery.

Cyril Smith

Apart from Eric Oliver, Britain's only other sidecar world champion of the 1950s was the popular Cyril Smith who conquered the world in 1952 despite a serious accident at Mettet the same year.

The former Army sergeant major was renowned for his toughness but could never really break out from under the shadow of his more successful compatriot. Sadly he took his own life in a Keswick hotel in 1962, an unjust end to the life of man who had given so much to the sport.

Like many sidecar drivers he first made a name for himself in grass track racing along with other famous sidecar personalities like Pip Harris and Bill Boddice. Many will remember his impeccable form at such Midlands grass track venues like Rushmere and Astwood Bank.

He made his road racing debut at Cadwell Park in 1949 and was soon to become a household name in threewheel racing. Despite making a name for himself on British and Continental short circuits, luck always seemed to evade him at the Isle of Man. He was well placed in 1954 but dropped out and the following year crashed on the first lap. This was the time in which the BMW drivers began taking control but Smith battled

well on his faithful Norton machinery and still managed sixth place in the world championship in 1957 when BMW's dominance was well advanced.

Of course in the 1950s the role of a professional sidecar racer was unheard of and Cyril's day to day job was that of service manager for a motor cycle business in Stockton-on-Tees. When he retired from racing he and his wife moved to Redcar near Middlesbrough.

When he died Cyril was 43 years old but his life could so easily have been brought to an end earlier during that practice crash in Belgium in 1952, ironically in the year he went on to win the world title.

He suffered a broken collarbone and fractured skull and quite amazingly was racing again just three weeks later when he finished runner-up at the Swiss Grand Prix. His other best world championship positions were a runners-up spot in 1953 and a third place in 1954.

John Surtees

When we look back through our history books the name of John Surtees stands out as one of the greatest of all time. Ask anyone who was fortunate enough to see this great man in action . . . his name stood for style, professionalism and unending dedication.

But while he scored with all these qualities on the race track he did allow his almost fanatical dedication to jeopardise his relationship with the racegoing public. He was not one of the most popular superstars in the history of the sport.

A fact which is often used to water down Surtees' achievements is that all his major successes came after the decision by Gilera, Mondial and Moto Guzzi to withdraw from road racing in 1957.

But very strongly in his favour is that marvellous sequence of results he strung together for his employers MV in the 1958 and 1959 seasons. During these two years he didn't lose one world championship event he entered. That meant that he won twenty-five 350 and 500 cc grands prix on the trot.

At the end of his bike racing career, he switched to four wheels in 1960, Surtees had won seven world championships (four 500 cc and three 350 cc) and won six TTs.

The legendary John Surtees. His name stood for style, professionalism and unending dedication. Pictured here with John Hartle

He took his dedication with him to the car racing world and to this day is the only man ever to have made the switch from two to four wheels and reach the top in both. Men like Mike Hailwood and Giacomo Agostini have tried to become world champions in the Formula I car world but failed. Surtees took to four wheels with the sort of class he had exuded in the world of motor cycle racing.

Born in Surrey in 1934 Surtees was given great encouragement at his chosen profession by his father Jack who was a successful grass track sidecar racer in his day. He ran a motor cycle business in Croydon and it came as no surprise to him when his son decided he'd go into the industry, beginning an apprenticeship with Vincent Motor Cycles at Stevenage.

His first road racing successes came on a 500 cc Vincent Grey Flash. Such flair did he show that he won his first race at Brands Hatch when he was only 17 years old.

Success at an early age continued for him and by the time he was 22 he was 500 cc world champion for MV.

Graduating from the Vincent he swung his leg over a Manx Norton and was so effective that he was given a works contract with Joe Craig's team for 1954 and 1955. In 1956 he signed for MV and repaid them by winning the 500 cc world championship at his first attempt for them.

That was just the beginning of a prolific career as a grand prix racer. In the three seasons 1958–1960 he was double world champion in 350 and 500 cc classes.

Surtees had one of the rare qualities in a top rider, that of being a first class mechanic and someone capable of analysing faults and transmitting information to the back up crew for a remedy. This greatly helped the development of the MV machinery which men like Giacomo Agostini were to inherit when Surtees moved on to motor racing.

His favourite British circuit was Brands Hatch and so successful was he there that he inherited the un-official title of *King of Brands*, a title which is now raced for at a specific meeting each season.

Percy Tait

Percy Tait is one of the real doyens in the history of British road racing and can boast a career which spanned three decades.

A test rider for the Triumph factory, Percy chose their products for most of his racing career and rode his first race on a Frank Baker prepared Triumph in the 250 cc class at the Silverstone Hutchinson 100 meeting in 1951. He finished second and that was to be the foundation of a career to last well over 25 years.

Now retired from the game with a farm in Stafford-shire and a car and motor cycle dealership in Birmingham Percy's efforts on British machinery were some of the best on record with a long list of prestigious titles along the way.

His first visit to the Isle of Man came in 1954 when he finished sixth in the Clubman's TT on a 500 cc BSA. The same year he looked set for third place in the Junior Manx Grand Prix when his machine developed gearbox problems.

He finished ninth in the Senior Manx of that year and first appeared in the TT proper in 1955 riding an AJS in the Junior and a Norton in the Senior which he crashed heavily at Hillberry.

Most of Percy's best remembered results came in the ensuing two decades.

Always smiling Percy Tait, now with long hair

Luigi Taveri

Luigi Taveri, the diminuitive Swiss rider was one of the best Swiss road racing representatives ever, whose illustrious career began in the 1950s but really came to fruition during the next decade.

His early world championship successes came on MV machinery when in 1956 he finished third in the 125 class and second in the 250 category. The following year he was runner-up in the 125 cc championship and then in 1958, having switched to Ducati he ended the season third at 125 level.

Taveri was one of those charismatic figures whom everybody liked in the paddock—a really cheerful character with plenty of style and professionalsim which was to stand him in such good stead during the 1960s when he joined Honda.

Carlo Ubbiali

Italian Carlo Ubbiali was one of the most prolific grand prix riders of the 50s winning 30 world championship races during this period.

A tiny figure of a man with plenty of grit and determination, he achieved world wide recognition in 1951 when at the age of 22 he won his first world championship—the 125 cc class on a Mondial.

This was to be the first of nine world titles which stood as a record until names like Hailwood and later Agostini went on to overtake this target. Ubbiali's magnificent tally of world titles comprised six 125 championships (one for Mondial and five for MV) and three 250 cc championships (all for MV).

Perhaps some idea of the sheer skill of the Bergamo rider can be gained from the fact that he didn't begin racing until he was 20 years old and showed so much promise that he was snapped up by Mondial and won them a world title just two years after his first ever road race!

Naturally his brilliant form secured him work with Mondial and he stayed with them for three years until he moved to the rival MV concern at Gallarate.

The presence of Werner Haas in the 125 and 250 classes at this time on the all-conquering NSUs meant that Ubbiali had a difficult initiation with MV but rode out the storm and when Haas and NSU disappeared from the scene he got back in his winning ways again.

Ubbiali, who retired at the end of 1960 at the age of 31, stayed with MV until his retirement and most of his world championship ratings were achieved thanks to a brilliant TT record dating from his debut in the Isle of Man in 1951.

During his nine year career Ubbiali made 15 starts in the Isle of Man and recorded five firsts, seven seconds, finishing outside the top two only once in 1959 when he finished fifth in the 125 cc race. The other two appearances are accounted for by breakdowns.

THE ROAD RACE CIRCUITS
OF GREAT BRITAIN AND EIRE

3

The meetings - the best of the racing

The championships Europe Great Britain
Belgian Grand Prix Dutch Grand Prix
French Grand Prix German Grand Prix
Italian Grand Prix Spanish Grand Prix
Swiss Grand Prix Isle of Man TT
Ulster Grand Prix

The championships

World championship racing in the 1950s was a far different proposition than it is today with the main difference being the number of rounds each season . . . almost six races fewer than today's grand prix scene.

Although the official FIM recognised world championship series did not originate until 1949 there had been a European series before the war but it originally had a rather unorthodox system of chosing its champions.

There was still a series of races for which riders entered but, up to and including 1937, the title of European champion went to the winner of a single meeting. Each year there would be a different host nation for the 'finals' day and it all depended on that day's performance as to whether a rider became the best in his class, regardless of whether he had won every other race that season.

A points system operated in Europe in 1938 and 1939 and when the FIM, who had overseen racing in Europe since its foundation in 1904, announced the world championships which began in 1949, it was again based on points so that the world champion would be the most consistent rider over the whole of the grand prix schedule.

During the early 1950s the grand prix season covered nine classic races. These events were the French Grand Prix, the Isle of Man TT races and then the grands prix of Ulster, Belgium, Holland, Germany, Switzerland, Italy and Spain.

But in 1955 there was a noticeable absentee, Switzerland. The horrific Le Mans car race disaster when a Mercedes caused a massive carnage frightened the Swiss authorities so much that they decided to ban the world championship race which had been held in their country since 1924.

So as grand prix racing entered the second half of the 1950s the line-up of races numbered eight with rounds in France, the Isle of Man, Ulster, Belgium, Holland, Germany, Italy and Spain.

Just for comparison there were 14 events in the 1981 world championship calendar. These took place in Argentina, Spain, Austria, Italy, Holland, Belgium, Sweden, Finland, Britain, Germany, Czechoslovakia, Yugoslavia and San Marino.

So you can see at a glance that the schedule was less hectic in the 1950s but then again travel today is much easier than it was in those days with superb motorway links between most European countries and of course far more advanced means of transport today.

There would be nothing unusual in those days for a privateer to hit the Continental trail with a car and trailer whereas today the more professional teams use fast, comfortable transporters equipped with everything from a kitchen sink to a luxurious stereo sound system to help pass the hours for the hardworking mechanics.

Few of the top names today actually drive from meeting to meeting. They catch a flight the day before practice is due to start and get a good night's sleep before the serious business gets underway!

Perhaps the dedicated men of the 1950s often wondered whether the stars of the 1980s would carry air tickets instead of spanners!

One of the other major differences between world championship racing three decades ago and that today was the method of awarding points for successes in grands prix. Today points are awarded to the first 10 finishers in any grand prix on a 15–12–10 basis but in the 1950s only the first six men home were rewarded. The scale of points then was 8–6–4–3–2–1 and the rider had to contest more than half the season's races to be eligible for the title. Such is the standard of competition today of course that no rider can afford to miss any race if he is seriously contesting the world championships.

In 1949 when the FIM was still feeling its way a little in terms of governing a proper world championship series points were only awarded to the first five riders home in a grand prix. The first man home got 10 points and those who followed him home received 8–7–6 and 5 points respectively. There was a bonus point for the fastest lap but this sytem was soon dropped in favour of the six best finishers system.

The latter system proved such a success that it remained in existence until 1969 when the current method of rewards was adopted. With a raising of standards and indeed a big increase in the number of riders seeking world championship fame there was an obvious need to spread out the rewards a little more to create a wider-spread incentive.

One thing which has not changed in 30 years is the demarkation between the privateer and the works rider. This became very apparent in the years soon after the official world title chase was introduced. The Championship carried more weight and therefore the manufacturers increased their involvement looking for prestigious marketing ammunition.

With a more meaningful goal to be had in motor cycle racing the manufacturers began investing more in their race programmes and of course all this was at the expense of the privateer who had been the predominant factor in those pre and post war years.

As time went on and the works teams began perfecting their products, wins by privateers in world championship competition became more the exception than the rule—indeed it is very much the same today with the powerful Japanese corporations ruling the roost.

But in the 50s it was the Italians, Germans and Britons who dominated the manufacturers' titles with the Britons sadly dropping out of contention as the decade wore on.

Examining the grand prix schedule as it stood in the 1950s it was altogether a more sensible arrangement in that it restricted its bounds to Europe. Today there are increasing demands from Latin American countries to stage events and quite frankly they simply turn out to be irrelevant farces with few more than the total number of possible points scorers making up the grid.

Costs are obviously prohibitive when it comes to organising grands prix in far off lands as the Venezuelan Grand Prix organisers discovered after two very questionable events which have forced them to put their world championship round on ice for the time being.

But back to the 1950s and the grands prix venues.

Many of the early road racing venues were sited on pure roads and pressure from a sport increasing in professionalism has meant the disappearance of many of these closed roads tracks.

But on the grand prix scene almost all of those early venues remain. Taking a look at the mid-50s calendar the actual grand prix locations were Reims (French GP), Isle of Man (TT races), Spa (Belgian GP), Assen (Dutch TT), Nürburgring (German GP), Monza (Italian GP) and Montjuich Park (Spanish GP).

Reims is no longer used for French road racing purposes having been superseded as a grand prix venue by Le Mans, with its 2.7 mile Bugatti circuit, and the ultra-modern Paul Ricard circuit in the deep south of France, without doubt the most modern circuit in Europe.

Of course history tells us that the Isle of Man was to lose its true world championship status after the 1976 races but the remainder of those 1950s grand prix venues are still in use today, apart from Montjuich Park in the centre of Barcelona which still hosts an endurance race but which lost its grand prix licence late in the 1970s.

Europe

Just as non-chapionships events are an important part of a riders programme today, in that they supply much needed extra income, so too were they highly regarded by the Continental circus members of the 1950s.

In addition to the nine world championship venues throughout Europe there was a thick network of purpose built and road circuits which would stage annual racing festivals, boasting the names of many, if not all, the main world championship contenders.

For those not fortunate to have a works contract these events helped meet the expenses of running around Europe to the vital world championship rounds. They made sorties to the Continent more worthwhile.

Looking at today's list of Continental venues and comparing it with that of 30 years ago the two have very little in common, save the existence of world championship circuits.

In France alone, for instance, there were well over 20 circuits to pick from, all of which staged some form of international competition during a season. Few remain on the international calendar today for the majority of this country's venues have been constructed since the 1950s. Names like the ultra-modern Paul Ricard circuit and Dijon spring to mind.

Working from north to south there were events at

Amiens, Caen, La Baule, Montlhèry, Rheims, Orleans, Rochefort, Strasbourg, Moulins, Vesoul, Mulhouse, Bordeaux, Clermont Ferrand, which reigned as a famous world championship venue until the mid-70s, Villefranche, Bourg, Tarare, Agen, Pau, Toulouse, Albi, Aix les Bains, Avignon, and Marseilles.

Spain could boast seven international venues whereas today only the two major centres of Barcelona and Madrid remain. The races of the 1950s were staged at Santander, Bilbao, Guipuzcoa, Pamplona, Saragossa, Barcelona and Madrid.

Holland's allocation of circuits was very much in keeping with today's with most events taking place at Assen and Zandvoort and an early international at Tubbergen. Indeed the Dutch government recently delivered a body blow to the network of predominantly road circuits by issuing a ban on their use following a series of appalling accidents.

Neighbouring Belgium had a plethora of circuits in sharp contrast to today's picture. Francorchamps was, and still is the nation's world championship circuit, but in addition to the road circuit in the Ardennes there were races at Mettet, Gedinne, Chimay, Seraing, Waremme, Floreffe and Sombreffe.

Moving on to Germany the head of their list, which still shares its world championship duties today with

SEE PAGE 114 *During the 1950s there were over 50 recognised road racing circuits in Britain. The Circuits stretched from Errol near Perth in Scotland to Ibsley near Bournemouth. Many of the Irish tracks still exist*

BELOW *Of this little group of circuits only Snetterton in Norfolk remains in use. The Norwich Straight is now redundant for motorcycle racing*

RIGHT ABOVE *Cadwell Park, in extended form, and Oulton Park still remain today. Racing recently returned to Aberdare but Brough is no longer used*

RIGHT BELOW *All these circuits remain today but the Hutchinson 100 has ceased to exist after a move from Silverstone to Brands Hatch*

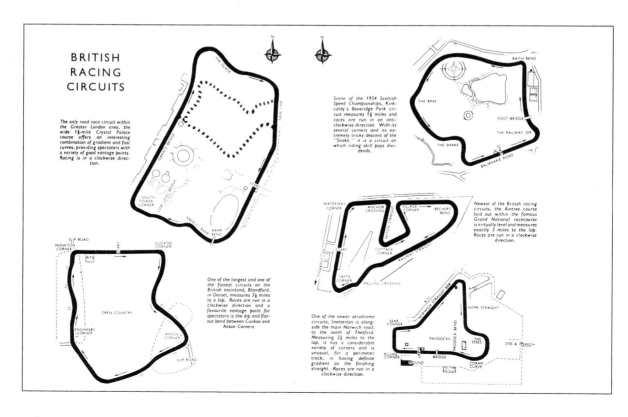

BRITISH RACING CIRCUITS

The only road race circuit within the Greater London area, the wide 1¼-mile Crystal Palace course offers an interesting combination of gradient and fast curves, providing spectators with a variety of good vantage points. Racing is in a clockwise direction.

Scene of the 1954 Scottish Speed Championships, Kirkcaldy's Beveridge Park circuit measures 1⅜ miles and races are run in an anti-clockwise direction. With its several corners and its extremely tricky descent of the "Snake," it is a circuit on which riding skill pays dividends.

One of the longest and one of the fastest circuits on the British mainland, Blandford, in Dorset, measures 3⅓ miles to a lap. Races are run in a clockwise direction and a favourite vantage point for spectators is the dip and flatout bend between Cuckoo and Anson Corners.

Newest of the British racing circuits, the Aintree course laid out within the famous Grand National racecourse is virtually level and measures exactly 3 miles to the lap. Races are run in a clockwise direction.

One of the newer aerodrome circuits, Snetterton is alongside the main Norwich road, to the north of Thetford. Measuring 2⅔ miles to the lap, it has a considerable variety of corners and is unusual, for a perimeter track, in having definite gradient on the finishing straight. Races are run in a clockwise direction.

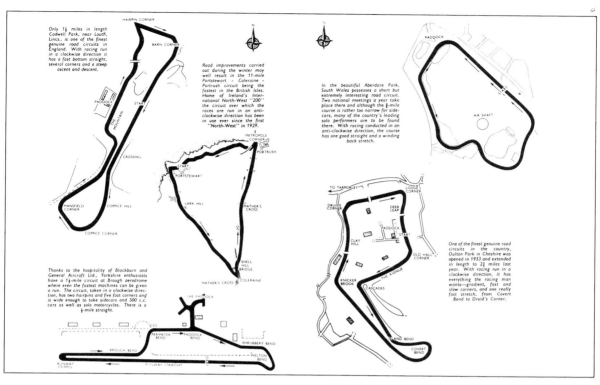

Only 1¼ miles in length Cadwell Park, near Louth, Lincs., is one of the finest genuine road circuits in England. With racing run in a clockwise direction it has a fast bottom straight, several corners and a steep ascent and descent.

Road improvements carried out during the winter may well result in the 11-mile Portstewart - Coleraine - Portrush circuit being the fastest in the British Isles. Home of Ireland's International North-West "200" the circuit over which the races are run in an anti-clockwise direction has been in use ever since the first "North-West" in 1929.

In the beautiful Aberdare Park, South Wales possesses a short but extremely interesting road circuit. Two national meetings a year take place there and although the ⅞-mile course is rather too narrow for side-cars, many of the country's leading solo performers are to be found there. With racing conducted in an anti-clockwise direction, the course has one good straight and a winding back stretch.

One of the finest genuine road circuits in the country, Oulton Park in Cheshire was opened in 1953 and extended in length to 2¾ miles last year. With racing run in a clockwise direction, it has everything the racing man wants—gradient, fast and slow corners, and one really fast stretch, from Covert Bend to Druid's Corner.

Thanks to the hospitality of Blackburn and General Aircraft Ltd., Yorkshire enthusiasts have a 1¾-mile circuit at Brough aerodrome where even the fastest machines can be given a run. The circuit, taken in a clockwise direction, has two hairpins and five fast corners and is wide enough to take sidecars and 500 c.c. cars as well as solo motorcycles. There is a ½-mile straight.

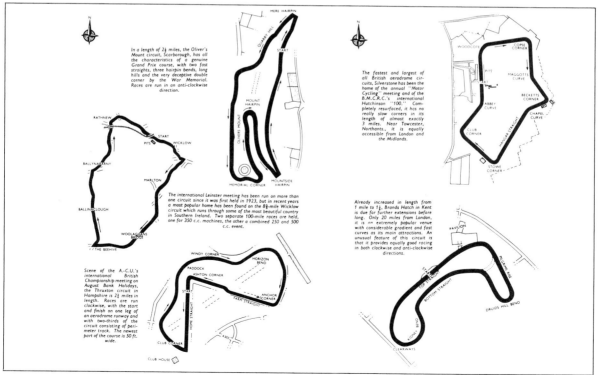

In a length of 2¼ miles, the Oliver's Mount circuit, Scarborough, has all the characteristics of a genuine Grand Prix course, with two fast straights, three hairpin bends, long hills and the very deceptive double corner by the War Memorial. Races are run in an anti-clockwise direction.

The fastest and largest of all British aerodrome circuits, Silverstone has been the home of the annual "Motor Cycling" meeting and of the B.M.C.R.C.'s international Hutchinson "100." Completely resurfaced, it has no really slow corners in its length of almost exactly 3 miles. Near Towcester, Northants., it is equally accessible from London and the Midlands.

The international Leinster meeting has been run on more than one circuit since it was first held in 1923, but in recent years a most popular home has been found on the 8¼-mile Wicklow circuit which runs through some of the most beautiful country in Southern Ireland. Two separate 100-mile races are held, one for 350 c.c. machines, the other a combined 250 and 500 c.c. event.

Already increased in length from 1 mile to 1¼, Brands Hatch in Kent is due for further extensions before long. Only 20 miles from London, it is an extremely popular venue with considerable gradient and fast curves as its main attractions. An unusual feature of this circuit is that it provides equally good racing in both clockwise and anti-clockwise directions.

Scene of the A.-C.U.'s international British Championship meeting on August Bank Holidays, the Thruxton circuit in Hampshire is 2¾ miles in length. Races are run clockwise, with the start and finish on one leg of an aerodrome runway and with two-thirds of the circuit consisting of perimeter track. The newest part of the course is 50 ft. wide.

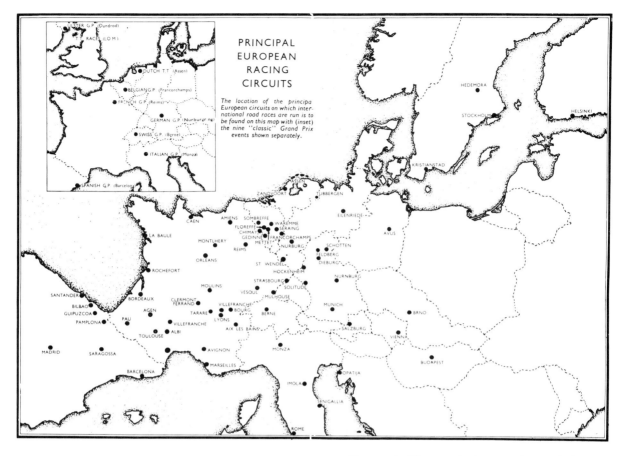

PRINCIPAL
EUROPEAN
RACING
CIRCUITS

*The location of the principa
European circuits on which international road races are run is to
be found on this map with (inset)
the nine "classic" Grand Prix
events shown separately.*

ABOVE *The network of European circuits was much greater in the
1950s. Many remain and have been replaced by newer, purpose built
circuits.*

RIGHT ABOVE *The Rheims circuit has since been superceded by such
tracks as Le Mans and Paul Ricard as a French Grand Prix venue.
But the Nurburgring and the Mountain circuit still survive. The
Clypse Course is no longer used*

RIGHT BELOW *Of these circuits Monza, Francorchamps and the van
Drenthe circuit at Assen still host world championship events.
Montjuich is now used for endurance events, the Ulster Grand Prix
lost its world championship status in the 1970s and road racing
is now banned in Switzerland*

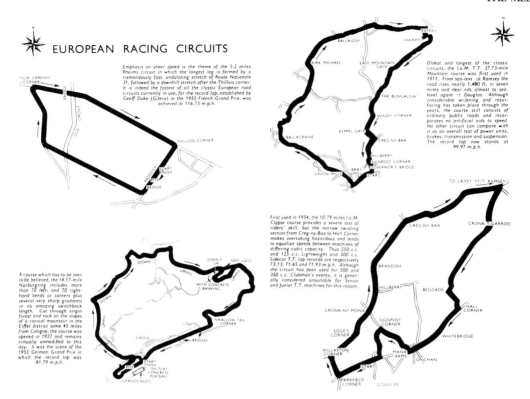

EUROPEAN RACING CIRCUITS

Emphasis on sheer speed is the theme of the 5.2 miles Rheims circuit in which the longest leg is formed by a tremendously fast, undulating stretch of Route Nationale 31, followed by a downhill stretch after the Thillois corner. It is indeed the fastest of all the classic European road circuits currently in use, for the record lap, established by Geoff Duke (Gilera) in the 1955 French Grand Prix, was achieved at 116.73 m.p.h.

Oldest and longest of the classic circuits, the I.o.M. T.T. 37.73-mile Mountain course was first used in 1911. From sea-level at Ramsey the road rises nearly 1,400 ft. in seven miles and descends almost to sea-level again at Douglas. Although considerable widening and resurfacing has taken place through the years, the course still consists of ordinary public roads and incorporates no artificial aids to speed. No other circuit can compare with it as an overall test of power units, brakes, transmission and suspension. The record lap now stands at 99.97 m.p.h.

A course which has to be seen to be believed, the 14.17-mile Nürburgring includes more than 70 left- and 70 right-hand bends or corners plus several very sharp gradients in its amazing switchback length. Cut through virgin forest and rock on the slopes of a conical mountain in the Eiffel district some 45 miles from Cologne, the course was opened in 1927 and remains virtually unmodified to this day. It was the scene of the 1955 German Grand Prix in which the record lap was 81.79 m.p.h.

First used in 1954, the 10.79 miles I.o.M. Clypse course provides a severe test of riders' skill, but the narrow twisting section from Creg-ny-Baa to Hall Corner makes overtaking hazardous and tends to equalize speeds between machines of differing cubic capacity. Thus 250 c.c. and 125 c.c. Lightweight and 500 c.c. Sidecar T.T. lap records are respectively 73.13, 71.65 and 71.93 m.p.h. Although the circuit has been used for 500 and 350 c.c. Clubman's events, it is generally considered unsuitable for Senior and Junior T.T. machines for this reason.

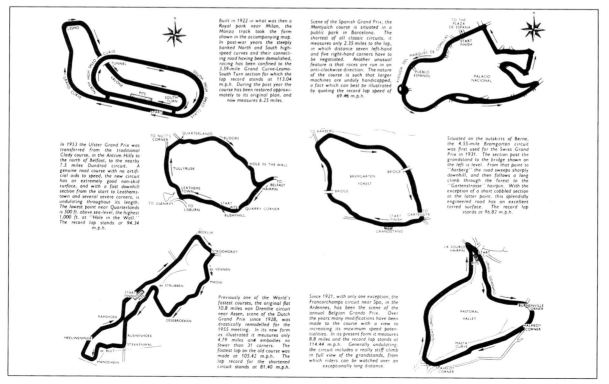

Built in 1922 in what was then a Royal park near Milan, the Monza track took the form shown in the accompanying map. In post-war years the steeply banked North and South high-speed curves and their connecting road having been demolished, racing has been confined to the 3.59-mile Grand Curve-Lesmo-South Turn section for which the lap record stands at 113.04 m.p.h. During the past year the course has been restored approximately to its original plan, and now measures 6.25 miles.

Scene of the Spanish Grand Prix, the Montjuich course is situated in a public park in Barcelona. The shortest of all classic circuits, it measures only 2.35 miles to the lap, in which distance seven left-hand and five right-hand corners have to be negotiated. Another unusual feature is that races are run in an anti-clockwise direction. The nature of the course is such that larger machines are unduly handicapped, a fact which can best be illustrated by quoting the record lap speed of 69.46 m.p.h.

In 1953 the Ulster Grand Prix was transferred from the traditional Clady course, in the Antrim Hills to the north of Belfast, to the nearby 7.5 miles Dundrod circuit. A genuine road course with no artificial aids to speed, the new circuit has an extremely good non-skid surface, and with a fast downhill section from the start to Leathemstown and several severe corners, is undulating throughout its length. The lowest point near Quarterlands is 500 ft. above sea-level, the highest 1,000 ft. at "Hole in the Wall." The record lap stands at 94.34 m.p.h.

Situated on the outskirts of Berne, the 4.55-mile Bremgarten circuit was first used for the Swiss Grand Prix in 1931. The section past the grandstand to the bridge shown on the left is level. From that point to "Aarberg" the road sweeps sharply downhill, and then follows a long climb through the forest to the "Gartenstrasse" hairpin. With the exception of a short cobbled section at the latter point, this splendidly engineered road has an excellent tarred surface. The record lap stands at 96.82 m.p.h.

Previously one of the World's fastest courses, the original flat 10.8 miles van Drenthe circuit near Assen, scene of the Dutch Grand Prix since 1928, was drastically remodelled for the 1955 meeting. In its new form as illustrated it measures only 4.79 miles and embodies no fewer than 31 corners. The fastest lap on the old course was made at 105.42 m.p.h. The lap record for the shortened circuit stands at 81.40 m.p.h.

Since 1921, with only one exception, the Francorchamps circuit near Spa, in the Ardennes, has been the scene of the annual Belgian Grands Prix. Over the years many modifications have been made to the course with a view to increasing its maximum speed potentialities. In its present form it measures 8.8 miles and the record lap stands at 114.44 m.p.h. Generally undulating, the circuit includes a really stiff climb in full view of the grandstands, from which riders can be watched over an exceptionally long distance.

Hockenheim, was the challenging Nürburgring. But other events were staged at Eilenriede, Schotten, Avus, Feldberg, Dieburg, St Wendel, Solitude, Nürnberg and Munich.

The Swiss circuit of Berne is of course defunct today since the country's ruling that no motor cycle racing, save that of hill climbing, shall take place but Austria's Salzburgring venue, complete with its superb natural amphitheatre is still a part of the world championship calendar. One Austrian location not on today's circuit directory is that of Vienna. There are several small internationals run in Austria during the year but the city of Vienna itself does not play host to any of them.

Brno is still the home of the Czechoslovak Grand Prix which attracts one of the biggest crowds of the season but now redundant, in terms of the European circus, is the Hungarian capital of Budapest.

Yugoslavia's former grand prix venue Opatija went out of fashion in the late-70s and so too have two of Italy's 1950s international venues at Senigallia on the east coast and Rome. The circuits at Imola, near Bologna, and Monza still remain.

None of Scandinavia's listed 1950s international venues remains today. The Swedish circuits at Kristianstad, Stockholm and Hedemora have all been superceded as has Helsinki in Finland.

Great Britain

The British road racing scene in the 1950s showed marked differences to that of today with the major difference being in the status of the meetings organised throughout the decade.

Today there are over a dozen international events in any one season but 30 years ago there were only four or five meetings of this standard. However national meetings of the day were of a much higher standard than those being organised in Britain currently.

National meetings in the 1950s could boast an entry comprising many of the national heroes. It would be nothing to see names like Surtees and Duke on the bill at a national event. This is perhaps equivalent to seeing Barry Sheene and Mick Grant at a national meeting today!

1950s action from Cadwell Park with the late Bill Boddice in charge. Bill later became an ACU steward

The Isle of Man TT races were the highspot of the British racing year along with the Ulster Grand Prix. Both of these meetings had of course world championship status in those days, having both lost their true world championship tag since then.

So there were in effect two British Grands Prix whereas today Silverstone hosts the only grand prix on a purpose-built track (a disused airfield) in contrast to the road circuits of the Isle of Man and Dundrod.

During the 1950s there were over 50 recognised road race circuits in Britain, considerably more than today and the TT and Ulster Grand Prix were backed up by the few international meetings, a healthy sprinkling of national and club events and the Manx Grand Prix and Clubmans TT held at the same time as the world championship Island series.

The big race of the year at Silverstone in those days was the *Motor Cycling* Silverstone Saturday which would attract crowds of up to 50,000 to see the likes of Geoff Duke and John Surtees doing battle.

In keeping with the standard of most of today's advertised internationals most of the big meetings did not live up to expectations in terms of entries from overseas, catering mainly for the big British crowd pullers and the occasional foreign privateer along with the Commonwealth rider who might be riding for one of the British works teams.

A typical series of internationals would take in Thruxton, Scarborough, Aintree and Silverstone. All these circuits are still in use although Thruxton and Aintree are not as prominent as the other two venues.

Indeed Aintree, which was opened in 1953, was probably the best purpose-built track in the country during the 1950s, having been commissioned by the famous race course owner Mrs Mark Topham. Famous for its top car meetings in addition to the best motor cycle events at that time the circuit is of course no longer in use in its former state. A scaled down version, which does not take in that section overlooked by the grandstands, is still used for club and national road race meetings.

Often on the bill at these major events would be championship deciders for the season. The organisers, the ACU would select one of the circuits to play host to the British championships, decreeing that they be decided in one day. Of course today's national championships, which don't carry the prestige of the 1950s style series, are run over a full season of national events.

An example of the interest from the stars in those days can be given by listing the 1955 British champions

John Surtees(1) leads a star-studded line up away from the Mallory Park grid in September 1958

who fought it out for honours at Thruxton that year at the August Bank Holiday meeting.

John Surtees won the 250 cc title on an NSU and also carried off the 500 cc crown on a Norton, 350 cc honours went to Bill Lomas on a Moto Guzzi and Eric Oliver was British sidecar champion that season . . . indeed that was to be his final year of competition.

All three champions were of course world champions at some time during their careers and there is no way you could say that about the British title contenders of today!

The British road racing season was roughly the same length as it is today, beginning on the first weekend in April and ending in October. Although there was not the amount of different clubs and their respective events, on average there were two meetings each weekend throughout the six month period.

Many of the circuits used for competition were airfields, there still being a plethora of concrete strips left over from the Second World War. Another large portion of the circuits, particularly in Ireland were pure road courses and the remainder were purpose built circuits like those at Brands Hatch and Crystal Palace in London.

Belgian Grand Prix

Until 1978 the natural road circuit of Spa/Francorchamps in the Ardennes mountains in Belgium, was the fastest grand prix venue in Europe. Then it was reduced in length from its original 8.8 mile distance and remodelled for safety reasons but it was in its existing state that riders in the 1950s became familiar with it. Just to grasp how fast the circuit was before it was altered its fastest laps in the late 1970s were in excess of 135 mph!

The long sweeping bends and the three mile Masta Straight were largely responsible for the incredible speeds the riders would reach. There were just two slow spots on the course at La Source hairpin, near the start and finish area, which still exists today and at Stavelot a village at the opposite end of the circuit.

The Belgian Grand Prix has been held at Francorchamps since 1921 and hasn't missed a year except in 1923 when the venue was switched to Dinant, 1936 when it was run at Floreffe and in 1980 when it moved to the Formula I car racing circuit of Zolder.

During the mid-1950s the lap record stood at 114.44 mph illustrating how machine development during the next 25 years added to the speeds riders were able to produce.

A typical Continental circus scene from the Belgian Grand Prix paddock at Spa in 1950, with a competitor working on his Norton ready for the race

Dutch Grand Prix

The van Drenthe circuit at Assen, scene of the Dutch TT since 1927, is today one of the world's best known grand prix circuits and one which attracts one of the biggest crowds to a world championship event each season, around 150,000.

The natural road circuit began the 1950s as a 10.8 mile course but in 1955 it was drastically changed, bringing its length down to 4.79 miles, the distance which remains today.

The first postwar meeting run at Assen was in 1946 and was restricted to Dutch riders. In 1947 it became part of the European championship and Britain drew first blood in the 500 cc class with a win for Artie Bell. Bell repeated his win the following year but that was to mark the end of the British domination.

Starting with Nello Pagani in 1949, the Italian factories went on to win every Dutch TT until 1965. In the 350 class Britain still held up its head and in 1951 Bill Doran scored a victory for AJS.

The magic 100 mph barrier was broken in 1952 by Italian Umberto Masetti on a Gilera and one of the most historic wins at Assen went to Geoff Duke on a Gilera in 1954 for it was to be the last race run over the 10 mile course. He lapped the circuit at 105.42 mph and of course that record stands to this day. Modern day speeds around Assen are much slower because the modified circuit layout includes more bends than in the existing design.

An example of how much more complex the post-1955 course is, can be gained from the fact that the fastest lap at the 1980 Dutch TT, set up by Randy Mamola, was only 97.15 mph.

Front row tension at the start of the 1956 Dutch TT at Assen. Nearest the camera is Tarquinio Provini with the works Mondial and next to him eventual winner Carlo Ubbiali (MV)

French Grand Prix

The French Grand Prix sited at Rheims during the 1950s and later moving on to Le Mans, Clermont Ferrand and Paul Ricard was the earliest 'classic' event on the European calendar and in honour of this its 'grand prix' tag was adopted by every other world championship race.

During the period it was used the Rheims track was the fastest in Europe and the fastest lap record for any Continental circuit was set up by Geoff Duke on a Gilera in 1955 at 116.73 mph.

Reason for its breath-taking speed was the extremely fast section of Route National 31 which formed part of its 5.2 miles length.

The first French Grand Prix was to have been run in 1914 but the outbreak of the First World War postponed the historic event. Eventually it took place in 1920 and was almost certainly the first ever grand prix to be staged. Of course at that time the British riders did little in the line of travel and so it was supported predominantly by Continental riders.

Most of the early events were run at Le Mans although when the Continental circus really came into its own Rheims became the most popular 1950s venue.

German Grand Prix

Held at both the Nürburgring and Hockenheim during the 1950s the German Grand Prix still graces these two circuits today on an alternate basis to keep the various organising bodies happy within the country.

The 14.17 mile Nürburgring circuit is one of the most famous and controversial in the world with its 150 tree-lined bends to be negotiated by the riders. It's a sort of mini-TT and of course in the 1950s when

every serious world championship rider contested the Isle of Man races the special demands of the Nürburgring didn't come as too much of a shock to the rider.

Today however the story is a different one. Ironically almost all of the grand prix stars who do not compete at

Action from the Sachsenring as Giacomo Agostini (MV) leads Alberto Pagani (Linto) and John Cooper (Seeley). East Germany no longer has a world championship race

the Isle of Man fare well at the purpose built circuit near Adenau.

After an initial spell on a circuit near Berlin the German Grand Prix was first held at the Nürburgring in 1927, the same year the German venue was chosen for the European championships. In 1953 the race returned to the Avus circuit on the outskirts of Berlin, a road circuit which is still used today for an annual international event which necessitates closing down a section of autobahn near the city.

From here the grand prix moved to the Sachsenring near Chemnitz which was later to be granted its own world championship race after the Iron Curtain split during the Second World War.

As already explained the Heidelberg circuit of Hockenheim was also favoured during the 1950s for the German Grand Prix, as it is today, but interupting the now traditional alternating rota between itself and the Nürburgring in the late 1950s came the 7.09 mile forest circuit of Solitude near Stuttgart.

But after a short stay at Solitude the world championship event was officially handed over to both the Nürburgring and the 4.8 mile Hockenheim course and has stayed between the two circuits since.

Italian Grand Prix

Traditionally the home of the Italian Grand Prix, although going out of favour in recent years for other venues such as Imola, Mugello and Misano, the Milan circuit of Monza has recently been given a new lease of life by the FIM, after being closed down following a spate of tragic accidents.

It was in 1973 that the legendary Jarno Saarinen and Renzo Pasolini were killed at Monza and a further accident at Italian national level finally closed it.

But now it's back on the grand prix calendar almost 60 years after its construction in what was then a Royal Park on the outskirts of Milan.

The circuit originally contained north and south high speed curves which were used in world record speed attempts but they were later demolished leaving the grand prix racing to be carried out on the 3.59 course which incorporated the Grand Curve and Lesmo South Turn section for which the lap record stood at 113.04 mph during the mid-50s.

British riders had a particularly good time at Monza during the 1950s winning no less than eight out of the 10 500 cc world championship races staged there.

Modena action in 1956 as Italian champion Libero Liberati (51) and Orlando Valdinoci test the 500 cc Gilera fours for the first time that year. The Monza track was still damp and so the factory chose the autodrome at Modena for their testing

LEFT *A close shave for Tarquinio Provini aboard the 125 cc MV at Modena in 1958 as he sweeps perilously close to the grass verge*

BELOW *Pit crews line the track at Monza in 1959 and cheer home the 250 victor Carlo Ubbiali on the MV who just got the verdict from MZ-mounted Ernst Degner who had earlier beaten Ubbiali in the 125 cc race*

Spanish Grand Prix

Montjuich Park was the original scene of the Spanish Grand Prix although it has faded out of significance these days for grand prix competition.

The circuit uses the existing roads in the beautiful Park surroundings but the 2.35 mile circuit became very restrictive for bigger machines as time went on with an average speed per lap during the mid 1950s of just under 70 mph. The course in a public park in Barcelona was the shortest of all classic venues during the 1950s with a total of seven left hand and five right hand corners to be negotiated by the grand prix competitors.

One of the circuit's unusual features was that races were run in an anti-clockwise direction which was in contrast to the race direction at every other grand prix venue.

But as the speeds of the bigger grand prix machines increased the Montjuich Park circuit became less and less favoured by the riders and today all Spain's world championship motor cycle racing events are held at Jarama on the outskirts of Madrid. Montjuich is still retained as a host to a round of the world endurance racing championship.

Grand prix riders battle it out for world championship points around the Montjuich Park circuit which in recent years has been deemed too dangerous for modern racing machines. It still plays host to endurance events

Swiss Grand Prix

Until the Swiss authorities banned road racing in 1955 following the Le Mans 24 hour car race accident, the 4.55 mile Bremgarten circuit on the outskirts of Berne, played host to the Swiss Grand Prix.

It had been the scene of the race since 1931 and was a public road circuit with a tarmac surface admired by most racers. When the circuit ended its days as a motor cycle racing venue the record lap stood at 96.82 mph, illustrating how fast it was.

From the start of the world championships proper British riders completely dominated the major classes at Bremgarten. From 1948 until the last race there in 1954 British riders won every 500 cc grand prix.

Harold Daniell was the winner in 1948 on a Norton and then Les Graham won the first two official 500 cc Swiss Grands Prix on AJS machinery followed by Fergus Anderson (Moto Guzzi), Jack Brett (AJS) and Geoff Duke who won the final two Swiss Grands Prix for the Italian Gilera factory.

Although, as today, the solo events took much of the limelight at grands prix the Swiss event did have a reputation for placing a lot of emphasis on their sidecar races.

ABOVE *Bruno Bertacchini in dynamic pose on his 500 cc twin cylinder Guzzi at the 1949 Swiss Grand Prix*

BELOW *A typical Swiss Grand Prix scene from 1950 as an up-and-coming Geoff Duke leads the field around the junction of Avenue de France and Rive de Lusanne. Norton mounted Duke is being chased by his fellow Briton and Norton rider Harold Daniell*

Isle of Man TT

Just like today, the Isle of Man TT races in the 1950s had a ring about them which put them head and shoulders above any other motor cycle racing event in the world. Ask anybody in the street what the Isle of Man is famous for or whether they have heard of the Isle of Man TT races and they are sure to give you the answer you are looking for. No other racing event in the world can boast the recall which the TT races have although the Isle of Man series today has no bearing at all on the world title chases. But going back 30 years nothing could have been further from the truth, everybody had to conquer the $37\frac{3}{4}$ mile Mountain course if they were to be in with a chance of winning the world championship.

The TT races have been the platform from which every major British manufacturer has built up their empires and in the 1950s the race was of premium importance to our home industry. Helped by the immediately postwar banning of superchargers on racing machines the British bike builders, who in the main had not joined the supercharging band wagon, really held their own.

The foreign factories furious at having wasted years of investment and research on adapting 'blowers' for their grand prix racers, took time to recover and had to bow down to British supremacy during this period.

The names Norton and Velocette were hardly out of the results during the first few seasons when peace returned but gradually the Italians and Germans began closing the gap.

The whole concept of the Isle of Man races was very appealing to the manufacturer. If his machine could come out tops after more than 264 miles of high speed battle over every kind of elevation then it had to be a good ploy with which to capture the public.

RIGHT ABOVE *Last minute check for a rider seconds before he starts the Senior TT. The start and finish area is identical today*

RIGHT BELOW *Mike Hailwood leads one of the few experimental massed start TTs down the Glencrutchery Road. Today the tried and tested interval method is used*

BELOW *Bouncing out of the saddle down Bray Hill, John Surtees wrestles the 500 MV to victory in the Senior TT. Surtees is pictured here in his heyday and was completely untouchable during this period*

The earliest of the Tourist Trophy races would have appealed to the manufacturers even more for they specified that only road going machines, in road going trim could enter the races. Therefore the exact machine which won the race could be bought over the counter.

There were also fuel restrictions. Single cylinder machines had to be capable of doing 90 mpg and twin cylinder entries were allowed to be a little thirstier at 75 mph. It may have been primitive but looking back it certainly made more sense than the heavy fuel drinkers which turn out today!

The Isle of Man course has remained, in principal, in the same format since 1911. The initial four years of racing were conducted on the St John's circuit which measured 15.8 miles which took in Tynwald Green, St John's, Ballacraine, Kirkmichael and Peel.

The 37¾ mile Mountain circuit was used for the first time in 1911 and hasn't changed, apart from surface of course, since then. In those days the fearless riders would have to negotiate several different kinds of road surface, including loose stones!

But by the 1950s the event had established itself as the leading road racing test in the world, and, by now of course boasting a tarmac surface all the way round.

Britain's near-dominance of the TT races which sandwiched the Second World War finally came to an end in 1955. The Italians and Germans had been creating a greater threat as each year went by. Then in 1955 Geoff Duke, the loyalist of British riders, who had campaigned well for Norton in those early 1950s, made the ironic breakthrough for Gilera, and took the Senior.

A look at all the class winners from 1955 will show us just how much Britain had lost its grip on the race series which had, for so long, been practically their own.

Duke won the Senior, Bill Lomas took the Junior on a 350 cc Moto Guzzi and was again winner in the lightweight event on a 250 cc MV, Carlo Ubbiali won the 125 cc race for MV and even in the sidecar class Britain were lagging. Walter Schneider won Germany their first ever sidecar TT with his BMW outfit.

Bill Boddice battled bravely for Britain to finish runner up on a Norton and Pip Harris crossed the line third on a Matchless.

And so the pattern was set for the rest of the decade. No British bike was to win a pukka class for the

RIGHT *Always a popular vantage point, the churchyard at Braddan Bridge a section to bring the best out of man and machine*

BELOW *Killed at Bray Hill in 1953, Les Graham races round the Mountain Course that same year*

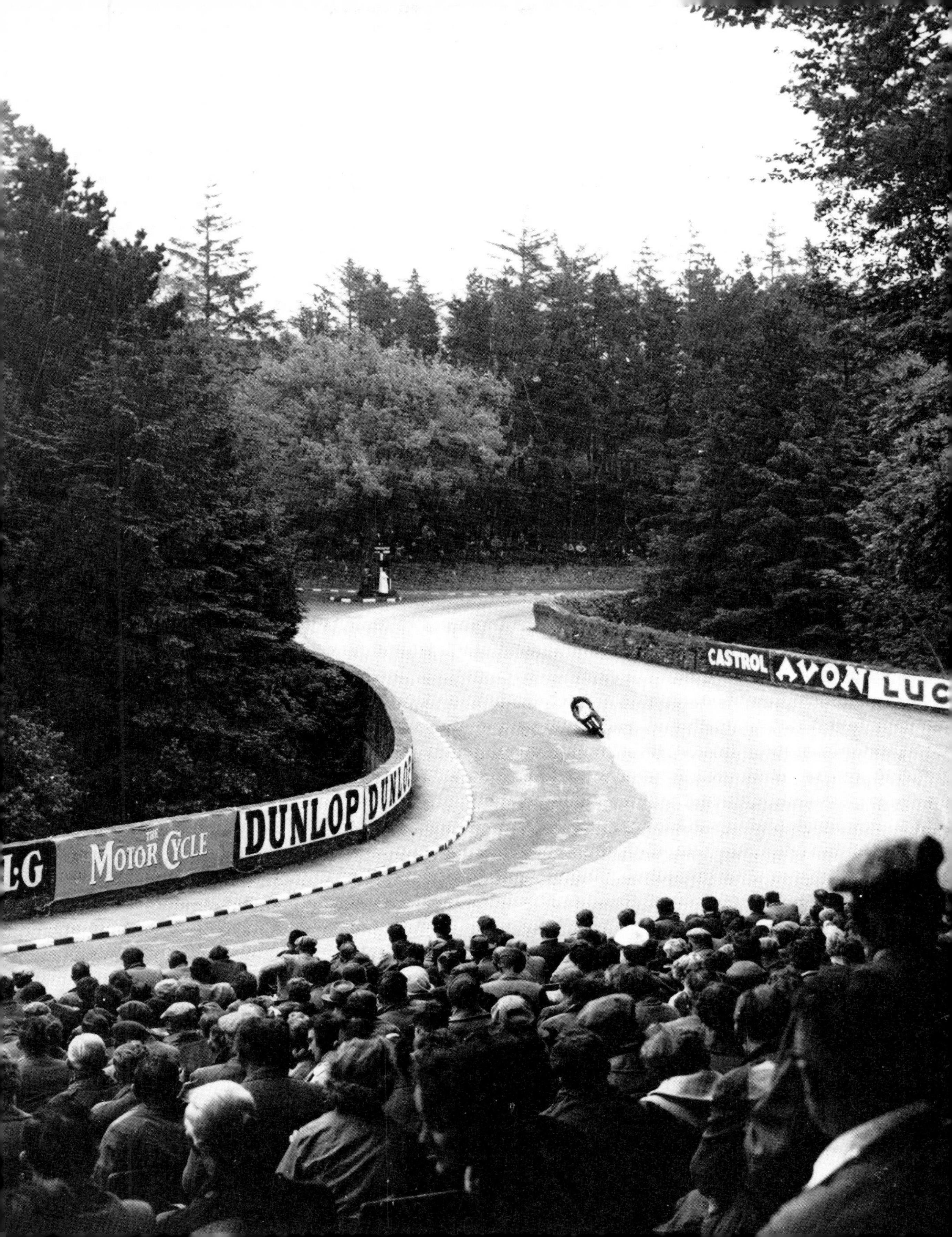
L·G
THE MOTOR CYCLE
DUNLOP
CASTROL
AVON

remainder of the 1950s. Bob McIntyre won the 1959 Formula 1 500 cc race on a Norton but this race was not in the normal world championship arena.

The British factories had lost interest by the middle of the decade as the increasing sophistication of the Italians strengthened its grip. Velocette did not support an official works team at the TT after the Second World War and Norton and AJS gave full works support at the British round of the world championship, for the last time in 1954.

It was sad but if you were a British rider and you wanted to succeed you could no longer be a loyalist!

The Italian domination continued relentlessly but when the shock news came in 1957 that three of the major Italian factories were to withdraw from the sport—Gilera, Moto Guzzi and Mondial—it did allow the British to get a little more of a look in. They didn't win any glittering prizes but had a steady stream of top three placings.

Still suffering for it today, it was MV, the Italian manufacturers who chose not to pull out of grand prix racing, who cleaned up in every major TT race between 1957 and the end of the decade. They are still accused of plundering in the absence of real competition but the TT wouldn't have been the same without them.

One of the major points of the 1950s was the introduction of the 10.8 Clypse course in 1954. This circuit, which incorporated some of the existing Mountain course was introduced to cater for those classes which did not attract the entry which the organisers felt warranted the use of the $37\frac{3}{4}$ mile distance.

The 125 cc, 250 cc and sidecar TTs were run over the Clypse course during its brief reign but after 1959 every class was again being held on the proper circuit.

But looking back at the 1950s in the Isle of Man the achievement during that period which must stick in everyone's mind must be the fantastic 100.12 mph lap set in 1957 by Bob McIntyre on a 500 cc Gilera.

It was the first time the 100 mph barrier had been broken and it is still talked about today as one of the greatest moment of TT history.

Heralding the Japanese invasion Honda works rider Taniguchi on a 125 cc racer at Nursery Bend on the Clypse Course in 1959

Clubmans

A regular feature during TT fortnight in the 1950s was the Clubmans TT, races for the lesser lights, run alongside the world championship races.

The ACU organising body worked the Clubmans races in with the TT programme. Entries for the Clubmans races were not too consistent and during 1955 they were transferred to the Clypse circuit along with the other less appealing events on the Isle of Man.

Many of the leading stars of the day entered the Clubmans races during their apprenticeship it giving them invaluable experience of the Mountain course with the atmosphere of world championship racing around them.

Manx Grand Prix

The Manx Grand Prix, held traditionally in September at the end of the Isle of Man tourist season, has always been a fine breeding ground for young road racers but as years go by and more and more pure road circuits become outlawed by both riders and authorities its meaning becomes increasingly diluted.

There was a time when you could look at Manx Grand Prix successes and pinpoint future world champions but that is not the case today. However there were one or two jewels among the 1950s roll of honour illustrating a greater importance in the 'amateur TT races' in those days.

Run over the same circuit as the June TT races the Manx Grand Prix was the ideal training ground for grand prix protégés, being run over a world championship course, no less.

The name Geoff Duke appeared as a winner in 1949 and other names which followed him throughout the 1950s who were to go on to greater things were Cromie McCandless, Robin Sherry, Derek Farrant, Bob McIntyre, Alan Shepherd, Eddie Crooks and then at the turn of the decade a youngster called Phil Read!

No such stars emerge from today's Manx races. The fact is that if a rider has an international licence he cannot enter the Manx Grand Prix and international licences are so much easier to come by that the number of Isle of Man first timers at the TT races has increased dramatically.

In its very early days the Manx Grand Prix would even receive works support from the British manufacturers, further illustrating the prestige it held.

Ulster Grand Prix

Established in 1922, the Ulster Grand Prix still stands out on the British road racing calendar as a meeting with something special. The challenge of the seven mile Dundrod course, the typically Irish paddock atmosphere and the unrivalled Irish hospitality.

The 1950s marked a definite period of transition for the event which during that time still enjoyed the world championship status which was to stay with it until 1971 when the FIM took away its grand prix lifeline.

What bigger change to undergo than the actual re-siting of the race which came in 1953 after the Antrim County Council announced that they would not grant the necessary road closing orders for the famous Clady circuit anymore. It was the end of an era filled with nostalgia as the unique road circuit with its world famous seven mile straight incorporated in its $16\frac{1}{2}$ mile lap, was made redundant. Before the Second World War the circuit had been $20\frac{1}{2}$ miles around.

Now the lap of the Ulster Grand Prix circuit would measure just over seven miles and after initial outrage by the local die-hards who couldn't imagine 'the prix' on any other track than the Clady the world championship event became well established and universally accepted.

All was not lost when the powers that be told the Ulster Grand Prix organisers that they would have to move home for it was at more or less the same time that car racing began on the Dundrod course and a pooling of resources and a sharing of costs became possible.

Dundrod, like the Clady course just a stone's throw from Belfast, was first used for car racing in 1950 when the Ulster Trophy event was held there. The little known youngster who won, was later to become somewhat better known as Stirling Moss!

That same year the motor cycle racing fraternity tried the course for size when the organisers of the long established 'Carrowdore 100' moved their meeting. However they decided to move it back to its original site two years later.

But whatever was said, the move to Dundrod was a successful one and it did have some lucrative spin-offs to offer for race organisers. In the days of the Clady meetings the organisers had not been able to charge for perimeter parking and therefore swell their funds. But with the move the Irish government, as if to soften the blow of having to move their roots, allowed the officials to introduce a payment system.

The first alteration to the actual programme at Dundrod came in the form of an increase in the number of races. Now there were five events, the increase coming with the addition of a sidecar race. At this time the racing was split between Thursday and Saturday, with practising having started on Wednesday. Thursday's races would include the 125, 250 and 350 classes with Saturday's concluding agenda containing the sidecar event and 500 cc finale.

In 1954 the organisers were experimenting again this time with the location of their meeting in the season's calendar. They felt that if they moved the grand prix forward from its usual August berth to June they might generate some interest from those at the TT and of course help out by making the sequence of events more convenient.

The year, unfortunately, will go down as one of the Ulster's worst. Main disappointment came from the weather—it rained non-stop as on so many other occasions and both MV and Moto Guzzi did not attend because of Isle of Man machine problems and a failure to reach terms with the organisers. So, as everyone might have guessed, the race went back to its original slot on the world championship calendar and has stayed there ever since.

In complete contrast the Ulster Grand Prix of 1955 enjoyed one of its beggest ever crowds, in spite of, as one journal reported at the time, the fact that Great Britain were playing the Rest of the World at soccer only a few miles down the road at a Belfast stadium.

That year the number of events was dropped from five to three but everyone had a good time at the trackside. Perhaps 1955's good attendance was the calm before the storm for yet again in 1956 the Ulster was having to cope with change.

The root of the next problem was the Le Mans 24 hour car race accident in which a stray Mercedes killed 80 members of the crowd at the French classic event. That horrific incident coupled with a series of car racing fatalities closer to home forced the RAC to wind up its car racing activities at Dundrod which featured two major events on the circuit each year . . . . the RAC Tourist Trophy and the Ulster Trophy.

The shock news left the Ulster organisers on their own. Nobody to share the costs with, they struggled on and indeed returned to a five race programme bringing sidecars and 125s back into play.

The following year there were changes again, although by now the Ulster Grand Prix was learning to live with an unstable composition. This time it was a decision to stage the meeting on just one day and therefore produce an altogether more economic approach.

The main difficulty was finding marshals to man the circuit during the week. People were less able to take four or five days off work to help the organisers and so this would be a way round things.

Sidecars again went by the board but the day's racing proved a success and the future pattern of the meeting had been set. Today's Ulster Grand Prix is a one day affair with the six classes taking up virtually the whole of the Saturday. Practice is held on Wednesday and Thursday evenings with Friday acting as a rest day in which to carry out repairs before the race.

LEFT ABOVE *Dickie Dale (BMW) leads Jim Redman on a Norton at Tournagrough during the 1959 500 cc Ulster Grand Prix*

LEFT BELOW *Siegfried Lohmann on a 250 cc Adler Rennsport on his way to eighth place in that class at the Ulster Grand Prix*

4

The Grand Prix results analysis

1949

Swiss GP

125 cc: 1 N. Pagani(I) Mondial 71.37 mph, 2 R. Magi(I) Morini, 3 C. Cavaccuiti(I) MV, 4 C. Ubbiali(I) Mondial, 5 U. Masetti(I) Morini, 6 F. Bertoni(I) MV.

250 cc: 1 B. Ruffo(I) Guzzi 81.21 mph, 2 D. Ambrosini(I) Benelli, 3 F. Anderson(GB) Guzzi, 4 C. Mastellari(I) Guzzi, 5 B. Musy(CH) Guzzi, 6 T. Wood(GB) Guzzi.

350 cc: 1 F. Frith(GB) Velocette 84.89 mph, 2 L. Graham (GB) AJS, 3 B. Doran(GB) AJS, 4 R. Armstrong(IRL) AJS, 5 T. Wood(GB) Velocette, 6 A. Bell(GB) Norton.

500 cc: 1 L. Graham(GB) AJS 88.06 mph, 2 A. Artesiani (I) Gilera, 3 H. Daniell(GB) Norton, 4 N. Pagani(I) Gilera, 5 F. Frith(GB) Velocette, 6 G. Leoni(I) Guzzi.

Sidecar: 1 E. Oliver/D. S. Jenkinson(GB) Norton 73.74 mph, 2 E. Frigerio/E. Ricotti(I) Gilera, 3 H. Haldemann/H. Laederach(CH) Norton, 4 J. Keller/E. Brutschi(CH), Gilera, 5 A. Milani/G. Pizzocri(I) Gilera, 6 R. Benz/M. Hirzel(CH) BMW.

Isle of Man TT races

250 cc: 1 M. Barrington(GB) Guzzi, 77.93 mph, 2 T. Wood(GB) Guzzi, 3 R. Pike(GB) Rudge, 4 R. Mead(GB) Norton, 5 S. Sorenssen(DK) Excelsior, 6 E. Thomas(GB) Guzzi.

350 cc: 1 F. Frith(GB) Velocette 83.08 mph, 2 E. Lyons (GB) Velocette, 3 A. Bell(GB) Norton, 4 H. Daniell(GB) Norton, 5 R. Armstrong (IRL) AJS, 6 B. Foster(GB) Velocette.

500 cc: 1 H. Daniell(GB) Norton 86.85 mph, 2 J. Lockett (GB) Norton, 3 E. Lyons(GB) Velocette, 4 A. Bell(GB) Norton, 5 S. Jensen(NZ) Triumph, 6 C. Stevens(GB) Triumph.

Dutch TT

125 cc: 1 N. Pagani(I) Mondial 68.84 mph, 2 O. Clemencich(I) MV, 3 C. Ubbiali(I) Mondial, 4 F. Bertoni(I) MV, 5 G. Matucci(I) MV, 6 J. Van Zutphen (NL) Eysink.

350 cc: 1 F. Frith(GB) Velocette 85.67 mph, 2 B. Foster (GB) Velocette, 3 J. Lockett(GB) Norton, 4 M. Whitworth (GB) Velocette, 5 E. McPherson(AUS) Velocette, 6 B. Doran(GB) AJS.

500 cc: 1 N. Pagani(I) Gilera 91.52 mph, 2 L. Graham(GB) AJS, 3 A. Artesiani(I) Gilera, 4 A. Bell(GB) Norton, 5 J. Lockett(GB) Norton, 6 H. Daniell(GB) Norton.

Italian GP

125 cc: 1 G. Leoni(I) Mondial 77.86 mph, 2 U. Masetti(I) Morini, 3 N. Braga(I) Mondial, 4 R. Magi(I) Morini, 5 C. Ubbiali(I) Mondial, 6 N. Pagani(I) Mondial.

250 cc: 1 D. Ambrosini(I) Benelli 89.57 mph, 2 G. Leoni (I) Guzzi, 3 U. Masetti(I) Benelli, 4 B. Ruffo(I) Guzzi, 5 C. Mastellari(I) Guzzi, 6 P. Castellani(I) Guzzi.

500 cc: 1 N. Pagani(I) Gilera 98.04 mph, 2 A. Artesiani(I) Gilera, 3 B. Doran(GB) AJS, 4 G. Leoni(I) Guzzi 5 B. Bertracchini(I) Guzzi, 6 L. Graham(GB) AJS.

Sidecar: 1 E. Frigerio/E. Ricotti(I) Gilera, 80.91 mph 2 F. Vanderschrick(B)/M. Whitney(GB) Norton, 3 A. Milani/G. Pizzocri(I) Gilera, 4 E. Merlo/D. Magri(I) Gilera, 5 E. Oliver/D. S. Jenkinson(GB) Norton, 6 J. Keller/A. Zellweger(CH) Gilera.

Belgian GP

350 cc: 1 F. Frith(GB) Velocette 89.72 mph, 2 B. Foster (GB) Velocette, 3 J. Lockett(GB) Norton, 4 M. Whitworth (GB) Velocette, 5 E. McPherson(AUS) Velocette, 6 R. Armstrong(GB) AJS.

500 cc: 1 B. Doran(GB) AJS 94.62 mph, 2 A. Artesiani(I) Gilera, 3 E. Lorenzetti(I) Guzzi, 4 A. Bell(GB) Norton, 5 N. Pagani(I) Gilera, 6 G. Leoni(I) Guzzi.

Sidecar: 1 E. Oliver/D. S. Jenkinson(GB) Norton 75.46 mph, 2 F. Vanderschrick(B)/M. Whitney(GB), 3 E. Merlo/D. Magri(I) Gilera, 4 R. Benz/M. Hirzel(CH) BMW, 5 P. Harris/ N. Smith(GB) Norton, 6 R. Rorsvort/V. Lemput(B) BMW.

Ulster GP

250 cc: 1 M. Cann(GB) Guzzi 79.98 mph, 2 B. Ruffo(I) Guzzi, 3 R. Mead(GB) Norton, 4 G. Reeve(GB) Rudge, 5 D. Beasley(GB) Excelsior, 6 R. Pike(GB) Rudge.

350 cc: 1 F. Frith(GB) Velocette 89.05 mph, 2 C. Salt(GB) Velocette, 3 R. Armstrong (IRL) AJS, 4 E. McPherson (AUS) Velocette, 5 W. Fry(GB) Velocette, 6 J. Swarbrick (NZ) AJS.

500 cc: 1 L. Graham(GB) AJS 96.41 mph, 2 A. Bell(GB) Norton, 3 N. Pagani(I) Gilera, 4 B. Doran(GB) AJS, 5 J. West(GB) AJS, 6 C. McCandless(GB) Norton.

World champions

125 cc: 1 N. Pagani(I) Mondial, 2 R. Magi(I) Morini, 3 U. Masetti(I) Morini.

250 cc: 1 B. Ruffo(I) Guzzi, 2 D. Ambrosini(I) Benelli, 3 R. Mead(GB) Norton.

350 cc: 1 F. Frith(GB) Velocette, 2 R. Armstrong (IRL) AJS, 3 B. Foster(GB) Velocette.

500 cc: 1 L. Graham(GB) AJS, 2 N. Pagani(I) Gilera, 3 A. Artesiani(I) Gilera.

Sidecar: 1 E. Oliver(GB) Norton, E. Frigerio(I) Gilera, 3 F. Vanderschrick(B) Norton.

1950

Swiss GP

250 cc: 1 D. Ambrosini(I) Benelli 75.99 mph, 2 B. Ruffo
(I) Guzzi, 3 D. Dale(GB) Benelli, 4 B. Musy(CH) Guzzi,
5 C. Bellotti(I) Guzzi, 6 O. Francone(I) Guzzi.

350 cc: L. Graham(GB) AJS 78.25 mph, 2 B. Foster(GB)
Velocette, 3 G. Duke(GB) Norton, 4 R. Armstrong(IRL)
Velocette, 5 E. Frend(GB) AJS, 6 D. Dale(GB) AJS.

500 cc: 1 L. Graham(GB) AJS 78.40 mph, 2 U. Masetti(I)
Gilera, 3 C. Bandirola(I) Gilera, 4 G. Duke(GB) Norton,
5 H. Daniell(GB) Norton, 6 J. Lockett(GB) Norton.

Sidecar: 1 E. Oliver(GB)/L. Dobelli(I) Norton 71.59 mph,
2 E. Frigerio/E. Ricotti(I) Gilera, 3 F. Aubert/R. Aubert
(CH) Norton, 4 H. Meuwly/P. Debaud(CH) Gilera, 5 W.
Wirth/F. Schurtenberger(CH) Gilera, 6 M. Masuy(B)/
D. S. Jenkinson(GB) BMW.

Isle of Man TT races

250 cc: 1 D. Ambrosini(I) Benelli 78.05 mph, 2 M. Cann
(GB) Guzzi, 3 R. Mead(GB) Velocette, 4 R. Pike(GB)
Rudge, 5 L. Bayliss(GB) Elbee, 6 A. Jones(GB) Guzzi.

350 cc: 1 A. Bell(GB) Norton, 86.31 mph, 2 G. Duke(GB)
Norton, 3 H. Daniell(GB) Norton, 4 L. Graham(GB) AJS,
5 E. Frend(GB) AJS, 6 J. Lockett(GB) Norton.

500 cc: 1 G. Duke(GB) Norton, 92.25 mph, 2 A. Bell(GB)
Norton, 3 J. Lockett(GB) Norton, 4 L. Graham(GB) AJS,
5 H. Daniell(GB) Norton, 6 R. Armstrong(GB) Velocette.

Dutch TT

125 cc: 1 B. Ruffo(I) Mondial 75.06 mph, 2 G. Leoni(I)
Mondial, 3 G. Matucchi(I) Morini, 4 N. Braga(I) Mondial,
5 F. Benasedo(I) MV, 6 J. Lagervey(N) Sparte.

350 cc: 1 B. Foster(GB) Velocette, 88.52 mph, 2 G. Duke
(GB) Norton, 3 B. Lomas(GB) Velocette, 4 J. Lockett(GB)
Norton, 5 R. Armstrong(IRL) Velocette, 6 H. Hinton(AUS)
Norton.

500 cc: 1 U. Masetti(I) Gilera 91.86 mph, 2 N. Pagani(I)
Gilera, 3 H. Hinton(AUS) Norton, 4 C. Bandirola(I)
Gilera, 5 E. McPherson(AUS) Norton, 6 S. Jenson(AUS)
Triumph.

Italian GP

125 cc: 1 G. Leoni(I) Mondial 82.09 mph, 2 C. Ubbiali(I)
Mondial, 3 L. Zinzani(I) Morini, 4 B. Ruffo(I) Mondial,
5 R. Alberti(I) Mondial, 6 E. Soprani(I) Morini.

250 cc: 1 D. Ambrosini(I) Benelli, 90.43 mph,
2 F. Anderson(GB) Guzzi, 3 B. Francisci(I) Benelli,
4 C. Mastellari(I) Guzzi, 5 A. Montanari(I) Guzzi,
6 V. Plebani(I) Guzzi.

350 cc: 1 G. Duke(GB) Norton, 94.98 mph, 2 L. Graham
(GB) AJS, 3 H. Hinton(AUS) Norton, 4 D. Dale(GB)
Norton, 5 B. Lomas(GB) Velocette, 6 C. Sandford(GB)
AJS.

500 cc: 1 G. Duke(GB) Norton 102.32 mph, 2 U. Masetti
(I) Gilera, 3 A. Artesiani(I) MV, 4 A. Milani(I) Gilera,
5 C. Bandirola(I) Gilera, 6 D. Dale(GB) Norton.

Sidecar: 1 E. Oliver(GB)/L. Dobelli(I) Norton 85.76 mph,
2 E. Frigerio/E. Ricotti(I) Gilera, 3 H. Haldemann/J.
Albisser(CH) Norton, 4 J. Keller/G. Zanzi(CH) Gilera,
5 E. Merlo/D. Magri(I) Gilera, 6 F. Muhlemann/M.
Muhlemann(CH) Triumph.

Belgian GP

350 cc: 1 B. Foster(GB) Velocette 97.26 mph, 2 A. Bell
(GB) Norton, 3 G. Duke(GB) Norton, 4 B. Lomas(GB)
Velocette, 5 C. Salt(GB) Velocette, 6 H. Daniell(GB)
Norton.

500 cc: 1 U. Masetti(I) Gilera, 101.16 mph, 2 N. Pagani(I)
Gilera, 3 E. Frend(GB) AJS, 4 C. Bandirola(I) Gilera,
5 A. Artesiani(I) MV, 6 H. Hinton(AUS) Norton.

Sidecar: 1 E. Oliver(GB)/L. Dobelli(I) Norton 82.50 mph,
2 E. Frigerio/E. Ricotti(I) Gilera, 3 H. Haldemann/J.
Albisser(CH) Norton, 4 F. Aubert/R. Aubert(CH) Norton,
5 A. Vervroegen/N. Verwoot(B) FN, 6 F. Muhlemann/M.
Muhlemann(CH) Triumph.

Ulster GP

125 cc: 1 C. Ubbiali(I) Mondial 77.44 mph, 2 B. Ruffo(I)
Mondial (only two finishers from seven starters).

250 cc: 1 M. Cann(GB) Guzzi 82.71 mph, 2 D. Ambrosini
(I) Benelli, 3 H. Billington(GB) Guzzi, 4 A. Burton(GB)
Excelsior, 5 G. Andrews(GB) Excelsior, 6 W. Campbell
(GB) Excelsior.

350 cc: 1 B. Foster(GB) Velocette 91.36 mph,
2 R. Armstrong (IRL) Velocette, 3 H. Hinton(AUS)
Norton, 4 E. McPherson(AUS) AJS, 5 C. Sandford(GB)
AJS, 6 H. Daniell(GB) Norton.

500 cc: 1 G. Duke(GB) Norton, 99.47 mph, 2 L. Graham
(GB) AJS, 3 J. Lockett(GB) Norton, 4 D. Dale(GB)
Norton, 5 J. West(GB) AJS, 6 U. Masetti(I) Gilera.

World champions

125 cc: 1 B. Ruffo(I) Mondial, 2 G. Leoni(I) Mondial,
3 C. Ubbiali(I) Mondial.

250 cc: D. Ambrosini(I) Benelli, 2 M. Cann(GB) Guzzi,
3 F. Anderson(GB) Guzzi.

350 cc: B. Foster(GB) Velocette, 2 G. Duke(GB) Norton,
3 L. Graham(GB) AJS.

500 cc: 1 U. Masetti(I) Gilera, 2 G. Duke(GB) Norton,
3 L. Graham(GB) AJS.

Sidecar: 1 E. Oliver(GB) Norton, 2 E. Frigerio(I) Gilera,
3 H. Haldemann(CH) Norton.

1951

French GP

250 cc: 1 B. Ruffo(I) Guzzi 85.07 mph, 2 Gianni Leoni(I) Guzzi, 3 T. Wood(GB) Guzzi, 4 F. Anderson(GB) Guzzi, 5 B. Lomas(GB) Velocette, 6 W. Gerber(CH) Guzzi.

350 cc: 1 G. Duke(GB) Norton 87.97 mph, 2 J. Brett(GB) Norton, 3 B. Doran(GB) AJS, 4 J. Lockett(GB) Norton, 5 R. Armstrong(IRL) AJS, 6 R. Coleman(NZ) AJS.

500 cc: 1. A. Milani(I) Gilera 99.17 mph, 2 B. Doran(GB) AJS, 3 N. Pagani(I) Gilera, 4 U. Masetti(I) Gilera, 5 G. Duke(GB) Norton, 6 J. Brett(GB) Norton.

Sidecar: 1 E. Oliver(GB)/L. Dobelli(I) Norton 82.24 mph, 2 E. Frigerio/E. Ricotti(I) Gilera, 3 J. Murit/A. Emo(F) Norton, 4 J. Drion(F)/B. Onslow(GB) Norton, 5 R. Betemps/G. Burgraff(F) Triumph, 6 A. Vervroegen/P. Cuvelier(B) FN.

Spanish GP

125 cc: 1 Guido Leoni(I) Mondial 53.55 mph, 2 C. Ubbiali(I) Mondial, 3 V. Zanzi(I) Morini, 4 R. Alberti (I) Mondial, 5 J. Bulto(E) Montesa, 6 A. Elizade(E) Montesa.

350 cc: 1 T. Wood(GB) Guzzi 58.32 mph, 2 L. Graham (GB) Velocette, 3 C. Petch(GB) AJS, 4 F. Aranda(E) Velocette, 5 J. Raffeld(B) Velocette, 6 J. Grace(Gibral) Norton

500 cc: 1 U. Masetti(I) Gilera 58.38 mph, 2 T. Wood(GB) Norton, 3 A. Artesiani(I) MV, 4 R. Montane(E) Norton, 5 C. Bandirola(I) MV, 6 R. Vidal(E) Norton.

Sidecar: 1 E. Oliver(GB)/L. Dobelli(I) Norton 50.25 mph, 2 E. Frigerio/E. Ricotti(I) Gilera, 3 A. Milani/G. Pizzocri (I) Gilera, 4 G. Carru/C. Musso(I) Carru-Triumph, 5 S. Vogel/L. Vinatzer(A) BMW, 6 M. Masuy(B)/D. S. Jenkinson(GB) Norton.

Ulster GP

125 cc9 1 C. McCandless(IRL) Mondial 72.23 mph, 2 G. Zanzi(CH) Mondial, 3 C. Clegg(IRL) Excelsior . . . (3 finishers only).

250 cc: 1 B. Ruffo(I) Guzzi 86.80 mph, 2 M. Cann(GB) Guzzi, 3 A. Wheeler(GB) Velocette, 4 T. Wood(GB) Guzzi, 5 D. Beasley(GB) Velocette, 6 N. Blemings(IRL) Excelsior.

350 cc: 1 G. Duke(GB) Norton 96.78 mph, 2 K. Kavanagh(AUS) Norton, 3 J. Lockett(GB) Norton, 4 R. Armstrong(IRL) AJS, 5 B. Doran(GB) AJS, 6 J. Brett (GB) Norton.

500 cc: 1 G. Duke(GB) Norton 95.48 mph, 2 K. Kavanagh (AUS) Norton, 3 U. Masetti(I) Gilera, 4 A. Milani(I) Gilera, 6 J. Lockett(GB) Norton, 6 B. Doran(GB) AJS.

Belgian GP

350 cc: 1 G. Duke(GB) Norton 100.08 mph, 2 J. Lockett (GB) Norton, 3 B. Lomas(GB) Velocette, 4 C. Sandford (GB) Velocette, 5 B. Doran(GB) AJS, 6 M. Featherstone (GB) AJS.

500 cc: 1 G. Duke(GB) Norton 106.66 mph, 2 A. Milani (I) Gilera, 3 D. Geminiani(I) Guzzi, 5 R. Armstrong(IRL) AJS, 5 N. Pagani(I) Gilera, 6 J. Lockett(GB) Norton.

Sidecar: 1 E. Oliver(GB)/L. Dobelli(I) Norton 82.24 mph, 2 E. Frigerio/E. Ricotti(I) Gilera, 3 P. Harris/N. Smith (GB) Norton, 4 C. Smith/B. Onslow(GB) Norton, 5 F. Vanderschrick/J-M Tass(B) Norton, 6 A. Milani/G. Pizzocri(I) Gilera.

Italian GP

125 cc: 1 C. Ubbiali(I) Mondial 84.52 mph, 2 R. Ferri(I) Mondial, 3 L. Zinzani(I) Morini, 4 C. McCandless(IRL) Mondial, 5 O. Spandoni(I) Mondial, 6 G. Matucci(I) MV.

250 cc: 1 E. Lorenzetti(I) Guzzi 89.29 mph, 2 T. Wood (GB) Guzzi, 3 B. Ruffo(I) Guzzi, 4 A. Montanari(I) Guzzi, 5 B. Francisci(I) Guzzi, 5 G. Paciocca(I) Guzzi

350 cc: 1 G. Duke(GB) Norton 97.93 mph, 2 K. Kavanagh (AUS) Norton 3 J. Brett(GB) Norton, 4 B. Doran(GB) AJS, 5 R. Armstrong(IRL) AJS, 6 R. Coleman(NZ) AJS

500 cc: 1 A. Milani(I) Gilera 105.13 mph, 2 U. Masetti(I) Gilera, 3 N. Pagani(I) Gilera, 4 G. Duke(GB) Norton, 5 B. Ruffo(I) Guzzi, 6 B. Doran(GB) AJS.

Sidecar: 1 A. Milani/G. Pizzocri(I) Gilera 89.38 mph, 2 E. Oliver(GB)/L. Dobelli(I) Norton, 3 P. Harris/N. Smith (GB) Norton, 4 H. Haldemann/J. Albisser(:H) Norton, 5 J. Drion(F)/B. Onslow(GB) Norton, 6 J. Murit/A. Emo (F) Norton.

Dutch TT

125 cc: 1 Gianni Leoni(I) Mondial 76.55 mph, 2 L. Zinzani(I) Morini, 3 L. Graham(GB) MV, 4 V. Zazni (I) Morini, 5 F. Bertoni(I) MV, 6 E. Mendogni(I) Morini.

350 cc: 1 B. Doran(GB) AJS 88.60 mph, 2 C. Petch(GB) AJS, 3 K. Kavanagh(AUS) Norton, 4 R. Coleman(NZ) AJS, 5 S. Sandys-Winsch(GB) Velocette, 6 B. Matthews (IRL) Velocette.

500 cc: 1 G. Duke(GB) Norton 95.67 mph, 2 A. Milani(I) Gilera, 3 E. Lorenzetti(I) Guzzi, 4 J. Lockett(GB) Norton, 5 J. Brett(GB) Norton, 6 V. Perry(NZ) Norton.

Isle of Man TT races

125 cc: 1 C. McCandless(IRL) Mondial 74.84 mph, 2 C. Ubbiali(I) Mondial, 3 Gianni Leoni(I) Mondial, 4 N. Pagani(I) Montlial, 5 J. Bulto(E) Montesa, 6 J. Liobet (E) Montesa.

250 cc: 1 T. Wood(GB) Guzzi 81.35 mph, 2 D. Ambrosini (I) Benelli, 3 E. Lorenzetti(I) Guzzi, 4 W. Hutt(GB) Guzzi, 5 A. Wheeler(GB) Velocette, 6 F. Purslow(GB) Norton.

350 cc: 1 G. Duke(GB) Norton 89.85 mph, 2 J. Lockett (GB) Norton, 3 J. Brett(GB) Norton, 4 M. Featherstone (GB) AJS, 5 B. Lomas(GB) Velocette, 6 B. Foster(GB) Velocette.

1952

500 cc: A G. Duke(GB) Norton 93.77 mph, 2 B. Doran (GB) AJS, 3 C. McCandless(IRL) Norton 4 T. McEwan (GB) Norton, 5 M. Barrington(GB) Norton, 6 A Parry(GB) Norton.

Swiss GP

250 cc: 1 D. Ambrosini(I) Benelli 74.39 mph, 2 B. Ruffo (I) Guzzi, 3 Gianni Leoni(I) Guzzi, 4 B. Musy(CH) Guzzi, 5 C. Sandford(GB) Velocette, 6 N. Grieco(I) Parilla.

350 cc: 1 L. Graham(GB) Velocette 80.44 mph, 2 C. Sandford(GB) Velocette, 3 R. Armstrong(IRL) AJS, 4 P. Fuhrer(CH) Velocette, 5 S. Mason(GB) Velocette, 6 L. Fassi(A) AJS.

500 cc: 1 F. Anderson(GB) Guzzi 80.16 mph, 2 R. Armstrong(IRL) AJS, 3 E. Lorenzetti(I) Guzzi, 4 C. Bandirola(I) MV, 5 B. Musy(CH) Guzzi 6 W. Lips (CH) Norton.

Sidecar: 1 E. Frigerio/E. Ricotti(I) Gilera 70.61 mph, 2 A. Milani/G. Pizzocri(I) Gilera, 3 E. Merlo/D. Magri(I) Gilera, 4. M. Masuy(B)/D. S. Jenkinson(GB) Norton, 5 E. Oliver(GB)/L. Dobelli(I) Norton, 6 G. Carru/C. Musso(I) Carru-Triumph.

World champions

125 cc: 1 C. Ubbiali(I) Mondial, 2 G. Leoni(I) Mondial, 3 W. McCandless(IRL) Mondial.

250 cc: 1 B. Ruffo(I) Guzzi, 2 T. Wood(GB) Guzzi, 3 D. Ambrosini(I) Benelli.

350 cc: 1 G. Duke(GB) Norton, 2 J. Lockett(GB) Norton, 3 W. Doran(GB) AJS.

500 cc: G. Duke(GB) Norton, 2 A. Milani(I) Gilera, 3 U. Masetti(I) Gilera.

Sidecar: 1 E. Oliver(GB) Norton, 2 E. Frigeriod(I) Gilera, 3 A. Milani(I) Gilera.

Swiss GP

250 cc: 1 F. Anderson(GB) Guzzi 85.08 mph, 2 E. Lorenzetti(I) Guzzi, 3 L. Graham(GB) Benelli, 4 A. Montanari(I) Guzzi, 5 N. Grieco(I) Parilla, 6 G. Gehring(D) Guzzi.

350 cc: 1 G. Duke(GB) Norton 91.54 mph, 2 R. Coleman (NZ) AJS, 3 R. Armstrong(IRL) Norton, 4 J. Brett(GB) AJS, 5 S. Lawton(GB) AJS, 6 R. Amm(Rhod) Norton.

500 cc: 1 J. Brett(GB) AJS, 93.76 mph, 2 B. Doran(GB) AJS, 3 C. Bandirola(I) MV, 4 N. Pagani(I) AJS, 5 R. Coleman(NZ) AJS, 6 R. Amm(Rhod) Norton.

Sidecar: 1 A. Milani/G. Pizzocri(I) Gilera 79.04 mph, 2 C. Smith/R. Clements(GB) Norton, 3 J. Drion(F)/I. Stoll (D) Norton, 4 F. Aubert/R. Aubert(CH) Norton, 5 M. Masuy/J. Nies(B) Norton, 6 J. Murit/A. Emo(F) Norton.

Isle of Man TT races

125 cc: 1 C. Sandford(GB) MV 75.49 mph, 2 C. Ubbiali (I) Mondial, 3 A. Parry(GB) Mondial, 4 C. McCandless (IRL) Mondial, 5 A. Copeta(I) MV, 6 F. Burman(GB) EMC-Puch.

250 cc: 1 F. Anderson(GB) Guzzi 83.76 mph, 2 E. Lorenzetti(I) Guzzi, 3 S. Lawton(GB) Guzzi, 4 L. Graham(GB) Velocette, 5 M. Cann(GB) Guzzi, 6 B. Ruffo(I) Guzzi.

350 cc: 1 G. Duke(GB) Norton 90.23 mph, 2 R. Armstrong (IRL) Norton, 3 R. Coleman(NZ) AJS, 4 B. Lomas(GB) AJS, 5 S. Lawton(GB) AJS, 6 G. Brown(GB) AJS.

500 cc: 1 R. Armstrong(IRL) Norton 92.91 mph, 2 L. Graham(GB) MV, 3 R. Amm(Rhod) Norton, 4 R. Coleman(NZ) AJS, 5 B. Lomas(GB) AJS, 6 C. McCandless(IRL) Norton.

German GP

125 cc: 1 W. Haas(D) NSU 73.05 mph, 2 C. Ubbiali(I) Mondial, 3 C. Sandford(GB) MV, 4 A. Copeta(I) MV, 5 H. Luttenberger(D) NSU, 6 L. Zinzani(I) Morini.

250 cc: 1 R. Felgenheier(D) DKW 77.84 mph, 2 H. Thorn-Prikker(D) Guzzi, 3 H. Gablenz(D) DKW, 4 E. Kluge(D) DKW, 5 G. Gehring(D) Guzzi, 6 A. Wheeler(GB) Guzzi.

350 cc: 1 R. Armstrong(IRL) Norton 81.00 mph, 2 K. Kavanagh(AUS) Norton, 3 B. Lomas(GB) AJS, 4 S. Lawton(GB) Norton, 5 E. Kluge(D) DKW, 6 E. Ring (AUS) AJS.

500 cc: 1 R. Armstrong(IRL) Norton 83.05 mph, 2 K. Kavanagh(AUS) Norton, 3 S. Lawton(GB) Norton, 4 L. Graham(GB) MV, 5 A. Goffin(B) Norton, 6 H. Baltisberger(D) BMW.

Sidecar: 1 C. Smith/R. Clements(GB) Norton 72.09 mph, 2 E. Merlo/D. Magri(I) Gilera, 3 J. Drion(F)/I. Stoll(D) Norton, 4 M. Masuy/J. Nies(B) Norton, 5 J. Deronne/P. Leys(B) Norton, 6 W. Noll/F. Cron(D) BMW.

Italian GP

125 cc: 1 E. Mendogni(I) Morini 84.39 mph, 2 C. Ubbiali (I) Mondial, 3 L. Graham(GB) MV, 4 L. Zinzani(I) Morini, 5 G. Sala(I) MV, 6 H. Luttenberger(D) NSU.

250 cc: 1 E. Lorenzetti(I) Guzzi 93.66 mph, 2 W. Haas(D) NSU, 3 F. Anderson(GB) Guzzi, 4 A. Montanari(I) Guzzi, 5 R. Colombo(I) NSU, 6 B. Francisci(I) Guzzi.

350 cc: 1 R. Amm(Rhod) Norton 97.59 mph, 2 R. Coleman (NZ) AJS, 3 R. Sherry(GB) AJS, 4 J. Brett(GB) AJS, 5 A. Goffin(B) Norton, 6 R. Schell(D) Horex.

500 cc: 1 L. Graham(GB) MV 106.29 mph, 2 U. Masetti (I) Gilera, 3 N. Pagani(I) Gilera, 4 C. Bandirola(I) MV, 5 G. Colnago(I) Gilera, 6 R. Armstrong(IRL) Norton.

Sidecar: 1 E. Merlo/D. Magri(I) Gilera 91.70 mph, 3 C. Smith/R. Clements(GB) Norton, 3 A. Milani/G. Pizzocri (I) Gilera, 4 J. Drion(F)/I. Stoll(D) Norton, 5 M. Masuy/ J. Nies (B) Norton, 6 F. Taylor/P. Glover(GB) Norton.

Belgian GP

350 cc: 1 G. Duke(GB) Norton 101.71 mph, 2 R. Amm (Rhod) Norton, 3 R. Armstrong(IRL) Norton, 4 J. Brett (GB) AJS, 5 B. Lomas(GB) AJS, 6 L. Graham(GB) Velocette.

500 cc: 1 U. Masetti(I) Gilera 107.12 mph, 2 G. Duke(GB) Norton, 3 R. Amm(Rhod) Norton, 4 J. Brett(GB) AJS, 5 R. Coleman(NZ) Norton, 6 N. Pagani(I) Gilera.

Sidecar: 1 E. Oliver/E. Bliss(GB) Norton 89.77 mph, 2 A. Milani/G. Pizzocri(I) Gilera, 3 C. Smith/R. Clements (GB) Norton, 4 E. Merlo/D. Magri(I) Gilera, 6 M. Masuy/ J. Nies(B) Norton, 6 J. Drion(F)/I. Stoll(D) Norton.

Spanish GP

125 cc: 1 E. Mendogni(I) Morini 57.66 mph, 2 L. Graham (GB) MV, 3 C. Sandford(GB) MV, 4 R. Ferri(I) Morini, 5 H-P Muller(D) Mondial, 6 L. Zinzani(I) Morini.

500 cc: 1 L. Graham(GB) MV 59.54 mph, 2 U. Masetti(I) Gilera, 3 K. Kavanagh(AUS) Norton, 4 N. Pagani(I) Gilera, 5 R. Armstrong(IRL) Norton, 6 S. Lawton(GB) Norton.

Sidecar: 1 E. Oliver/E. Bliss(GB) Norton 53.79 mph, 2 J. Drion(F)/I. Stoll(D) Norton, 3 C. Smith/R. Clements (GB) Norton, 4 O. Schmid/O. Kolle(D) Norton, 5 R. Betemps/A. Drivet(F) Triumph, 6 R. Koch/A. Flach (D) BMW.

Ulster GP

125 cc: 1 C. Sandford(GB) MV 77.39 mph, 2 B. Lomas (GB) MV, 3 C. Salt(GB) MV . . . 3 finishers from 8 starters

250 cc: 1 M. Cann(GB) Guzzi 86.16 mph, 2 E. Lorenzetti (I) Guzzi, 3 L. Graham(GB) Velocette, 4 R. Mead(GB) Velocette, 5 B. Rood(GB) Velocette, 6 R. Petty(GB) Norton.

350 cc: 1 K. Kavanagh(AUS) Norton 94.82 mph, 2 R. Armstrong(IRL) Norton, 3 R. Coleman(NZ) AJS, 4 J. Brett (GB) AJS, 5 E. Ring(AUS) AJS, 6 M. O'Rourke(GB) AJS.

500 cc: 1 C. McCandless(IRL) Gilera 99.73 mph, 2 R. Coleman(NZ) AJS, 3 B. Lomas(GB) MV, 4 J. Brett (GB) AJS, 5 Ph. Carter(GB) Norton, 6 J. Surtees(GB) Norton.

Dutch GP

125 cc: 1 C. Sandford(GB) MV 78.79 mph, 2 C. Ubbiali (I) Mondial, 3 L. Zinzani(I) Morini, 4 G. Sala(I) MV, 5 A. Copeta(I) MV, 6 L. Simmons(Holl) Mondial.

250 cc: 1 E. Lorenzetti(I) Guzzi 84.98 mph, 2 B. Ruffo(I) Guzzi, 3 F. Anderson(GB) Guzzi, 4 A. Wheeler(GB) Guzzi, 5 B. Webster(GB) Velocette, 6 S. Postma(Holl) Guzzi.

350 cc: 1 G. Duke(GB) Norton 92.97 mph, 2 R. Amm (Rhod) Norton, 3 R. Coleman(NZ) AJS, 4 R. Armstrong (IRL) Norton, 5 K. Kavanagh(AUS) Norton, 6 J. Brett (GB) AJS.

500 cc: 1 U. Masetti(I) Gilera 97.16 mph, 2 G. Duke(GB) Norton, 3 K. Kavanagh(AUS) Norton, 4 R. Armstrong (IRL) Norton, 5 R. Coleman(NZ) AJS, 6 N. Pagani(I) Gilera.

World champions

125 cc: 1 C. Sandford(GB) MV, 2 C. Ubbiali(I) Mondial, 3 E. Mendogni(I) Morini.

250 cc: 1 E. Lorenzetti(I) Guzzi, 2 F. Anderson(GB) Guzzi, 3 L. Graham(GB) Velocette.

350 cc: 1 G. Duke(GB) Norton, 2 R. Armstrong(IRL) Norton, 3 R. Amm(Rhod) Norton.

500 cc: 1 U. Masetti(I) Gilera, 2 L. Graham(GB) MV, 3 R. Armstrong(IRL) Norton.

Sidecar: 1 C. Smith(GB) Norton, 2 A. Milani(I) Gilera, 3 J. Drion(F) Norton.

1953

Dutch GP

125 cc: 1 W. Haas(D) NSU 78.85 mph, 2 C. Ubbiali(I) MV, 3 C. Sandford(GB) MV, 4 L. Zinzani(I) Morini, 5 H. Veer (NL) Morini, 6 L. Simmons(NL) Mondial.

250 cc: 1 W. Haas(D) NSU 91.27 mph, 2 F. Anderson(GB) Guzzi, 3 R. Armstrong(IRL) Guzzi, 4 E. Lorenzetti(I) Guzzi, 5 S. Wunsche(D) DKW, 6 A. Hobl(D, DKW.

350 cc: 1 E. Lorenzetti(I) Guzzi 93.43 mph, 2 R. Amm (Rhod) Norton, 3 K. Kavanagh(AUS) Norton, 4 J. Brett (GB) Norton, 5 E. Ring(A) AJS, 6 B. Doran(GB) AJS.

500 cc: 1 G. Duke(GB) Gilera 99.91 mph, 2 R. Armstrong (IRL) Gilera, 3 K. Kavanagh(AUS) Norton, 4 G. Colnago (I) Gilera, 5 J. Brett(GB) Norton, 6 B. Doran(GB) AJS.

German GP

125 cc: 1 C. Ubbiali(I) MV 69.24 mph, 2 W. Haas(D) NSU, 3 O. Daiker(D) NSU, 4 A. Copeta(I) MV, 5 W. Reichert(D) NSU, 6 K. Lottes(D) MW.

250 cc: 1 W. Haas(D) NSU 74.39 mph, 2 A. Montanari(I) Guzzi, 3 A. Hobl(D) DKW, 4 W. Reichert(D) NSU, 5 O. Daiker(D) NSU, 6 R. Hollaus(A) Guzzi.

Ulster GP

125 cc: 1 W. Haas(D) NSU 74.85 mph, 2 C. Sandford(GB) MV, 3 R. Armstrong(IRL) NSU, 4 O. Daiker(D) NSU, 5 T. Forconi(I) MV, 6 F. Purslow(GB) MV.

250 cc: 1 R. Armstrong(IRL) NSU 81.74 mph, 2 W. Haas (D) NSU, 3 F. Anderson(GB) Guzzi, 4 E. Lorenzetti(I) Guzzi, 5 O. Daiker(D) NSU, 6 A. Wheeler(GB) Guzzi.

350 cc: 1 K. Mudford(NZ) Norton 83.99 mph, 2 B. McIntyre(GB) AJS, 3 R. Coleman(NZ) AJS, 4 H. Pearce (GB) Velocette, 5 M. Templeton(GB) AJS, 6 K. Harwood (GB) AJS.

500 cc: 1 K. Kavanagh(AUS) Norton 89.79 mph, 2 G. Duke (GB) Gilera, 3 J. Brett(GB) Norton, 4 R. Armstrong(IRL) Gilera, 5 D. Farrant(GB) AJS, 6 K. Mudford(NZ) Norton.

Sidecar: 1 C. Smith/R. Clements(GB) Norton 77.73 mph, 2 P. Harris/R. Campbell(GB) Norton, 3 J. Drion(F)/I. Stoll (D) Norton, 4 T. Bounds/R. King(IRL) Norton, 5 F. Purslow/F. Kay(GB) BSA . . . only 5 finishers from 7 starters.

Italian GP

125 cc: 1 W. Haas(D) NSU 86.97 mph, 2 E. Mendogni(I) Morini, 3 C. Ubbiali(I) MV, 4 A. Copeta(I) MV, 5 W. Brandt(D) NSU, 6 P. Campanelli(I) MV.

250 cc: 1 E. Lorenzetti(I) Guzzi 98.51 mph, 2 W. Haas(D) NSU, 3 A. Montanari(I) Guzzi, 4 R. Armstrong(IRL) NSU, 5 W. Brandt(D) NSU, 6 U. Masetti(I) NSU.

350 cc: 1 E. Lorenzetti(I) Guzzi 99.54 mph, 2 F. Anderson (GB) Guzzi, 3 D. Agostini(I) Guzzi, 4 A. Hobl(D) DKW, 5 L. Simpson(NZ) AJS, 6 T. McAlpine(AUS) Norton.

500 cc: 1 G. Duke(GB) Gilera 106.84 mph, 2 D. Dale(GB) Gilera, 3 L. Liberati(I) Gilera, 4 R. Armstrong(IRL) Gilera, 5 C. Sandford(GB) MV, 6 H-P Muller(D) MV.

Sidecar: 1 E. Oliver/S. Dibben(GB) Norton 88.77 mph, 2 C. Smith/R. Clements(GB) Norton, 3 J. Drion(F)/I. Stoll(D) Norton, 4 H. Haldemann/J. Albisser(CH) Norton, 5 F. Taylor/P. Glover(GB) Norton, 6 F. Hillebrand/M. Grunwald(D) BMW.

Spanish GP

125 cc: 1 A. Copeta(I) MV 59.34 mph, 2 C. Sandford(GB) MV, 3 R. Hollaus(A) NSU, 4 W. Brandt(D) NSU, 5 M. Cama(E) Montesa, 6 G. Braun(D) Mondial.

250 cc: 1 E. Lorenzetti(I) Guzzi 57.87 mph, 2 K. Kavanagh(AUS) Guzzi, 3 F. Anderson(GB) Guzzi, 4 A. Montanari(I) Guzzi, 5 T. Wood(GB) Guzzi, 6 A. Hobl(D) DKW.

500 cc: 1 F. Anderson(GB) Guzzi 59.99 mph, 2 C. Bandirola(I) MV, 3 D. Dale(GB) Gilera, 4 G. Colnago (I) Gilera, 5 N. Pagani(I) Gilera, 6 T. Wood(GB) Norton.

Swiss GP

250 cc: 1 R. Armstrong(IRL) NSU 88.30 mph, 2 A. Montanari(I) Guzzi, 3 F. Anderson(GB) Guzzi, 4 E. Lorenzetti(I) Guzzi, 5 O. Daiker(D) NSU, 6 W. Haas(D) NSU.

350 cc: 1 F. Anderson(GB) Guzzi 90.67 mph, 2 K. Kavanagh(AUS) Norton, 3 R. Coleman(NZ) AJS, 4 J. Brett(GB) Norton, 5 D. Farrant(GB) AJS, 6 K. Hoffman(D) DKW.

500 cc: 1 G. Duke(GB) Gilera 98.12 mph, 2 A. Milani(I) Gilera, 3 R. Armstrong(IRL) Gilera, 4 G. Colnago(I) Gilera, 5 R. Coleman(NZ) AJS, 6 D. Farrant(GB) AJS.

Sidecar: 1 E. Oliver/S. Dibben(GB) Norton 82.42 mph, 2 C. Smith/R. Clements(GB) Norton, 3 W. Noll/F. Cron (D) BMW, 4 H. Haldemann/J. Albisser(CH) Norton, 5 J. Drion(F)/I. Stoll(D) Norton, 6 J. Deronne/P. Leys ((B) Norton.

Belgian GP

350 cc: 1 F. Anderson(GB) Guzzi 103.31 mph, 2 E. Lorenzetti(I) Guzzi, 3 R. Amm(Rhod) Norton, 4 J. Brett(GB) Norton, 5 K. Kavanagh(AUS) Norton, 6 R. Coleman(NZ) AJS.

500 cc: 1 A. Milani(I) Gilera 110.16 mph, 2 R. Amm(Rhod) (Norton, 3 R. Armstrong(IRL) Gilera, 4 K. Kavanagh(AUS) Norton, 5 R. Coleman(NZ) AJS, 6 D. Dale(GB) Gilera.

Sidecar: 1 E. Oliver/S. Dibben(GB) Norton 90.54 mph, 2 C. Smith/B. Onslow(GB) Norton, 3 W. Krauss/B. Huser (D) BMW, 4 M. Masuy/J. Nies(B) Norton, 5 H. Haldemann/J. Albisser(CH) Norton, 6 W. Noll/F. Cron(D) BMW.

1954

Isle of Man TT races

125 cc: 1 L. Graham(GB) MV 77.74 mph, 2 W. Haas(D) NSU, 3 C. Sanderford(GB) MV, 4 A. Copeta(I) MV, 5 A. Jones(GB) MV, 6 B. Webster(GB) MV.

250 cc: 1 F. Anderson(GB) Guzzi 84.67 mph, 2 W. Haas (D) NSU, 3 S. Wuensche(D) DKW, 4 A. Wheeler(GB) Guzzi, 5 S. Willis(AUS) Velocette, 6 T. Wood(GB) Guzzi.

350 cc: 1 R. Amm(Rhod) Norton 90.46 mph, 2 K. Kavanagh(AUS) Norton, 3 F. Anderson(GB) Guzzi, 4 J. Brett(GB) Norton, 5 B. Doran(GB) AJS, 6 D. Farrant (GB) AJS.

500 cc: 1 R. Amm(Rhod) Norton 93.79 mph, 2 J. Brett (GB) Norton, 3 R. Armstrong(IRL) Gilera, 4 R. Coleman (NZ) AJS, 5 B. Doran(GB) AJS, 6 P. Davey(GB) Norton.

World champions

125 cc: 1 W. Haas(D) NSU, 2 C. Sandford(GB) MV, 3 C. Ubbiali(I) MV.

250 cc: 1 W. Haas(D) NSU, 2 R. Armstrong(IRL) NSU, 3 F. Anderson(GB) Guzzi.

350 cc: 1 F. Anderson(GB) Guzzi, 2 E. Lorenzetti(I) Guzzi, 3 R. Amm(Rhod) Norton.

500 cc: 1 G. Duke(GB) Gilera, 2 R. Armstrong(IRL) Gilera, 3 A. Milani(I) Gilera.

Sidecar: 1 E. Oliver(GB) Norton, 2 C. Smith(GB) Norton, 3 H. Haldemann(CH) Norton.

Isle of Man TT races

125 cc: 1 R. Hollaus(A) NSU 69.52 mph, 2 C. Ubbiali (I) MV, 3 C. Sandford(GB) MV, 4 H. Baltisberger(D) NSU, 5 J. Lloyd(GB) MV, 6 F. Purslow(GB) MV.

250 cc: 1 W. Haas(D) NSU 90.83 mph, 2 R. Hollaus(A) NSU, 3 R. Armstrong(IRL) NSU, 4 H-P Muller(D) NSU, 5 F. Anderson(GB) Guzzi, 6 H. Baltisberger(D) NSU.

350 cc: 1 R. Coleman(NZ) AJS 91.44 mph, 2 D. Farrant (GB) AJS, 3 R. Keeler(GB) Norton, 4 L. Simpson(NZ) AJS, 5 P. Davey(GB) Norton, 6 J. Clark(GB) AJS.

500 cc: 1 R. Amm(Rhod) Norton 88.06 mph, 2 G. Duke (GB) Gilera, 3 J. Brett(GB) Norton, 4 R. Armstrong(IRL) Gilera, 5 R. Allison(SA) Norton, 6 G. Laing(AUS) Norton.

Sidecar: 1 E. Oliver/L. Nutt(GB) Norton 68.82 mph, 2 F. Hillebrand/M. Grunwald(D) BMW, 3 W. Noll/F. Cron(D) BMW, 4 W. Schneider/H. Strauss(D) BMW, 5 J. Drion(F)/I. Stoll(D) Norton, 6 B. Boddice/J. Pirie(GB) Norton.

Ulster GP

125 cc: 1 R. Hollaus(A) NSU 76.95 mph, 2 H-P Muller(D) NSU, 3 H. Baltisberger(D) NSU, 4 W. Haas(D) NSU, 5 C. Sandford(GB) MV, 6 A. Copeta(I) MV.

250 sc: 1 W. Haas(D) 77.85 mph, 2 H. Baltisberger(D) NSU, 3 H-P Muller(D) NSU, 4 A. Wheeler(GB) Guzzi, 5 J. Horne(GB) Rudge, 6 R. Geeson(GB) REG.

350 cc: 1 R. Amm(Rhod) Norton 83.40 mph, 2 J. Brett (GB) Norton, 3 B. McIntyre(GB) AJS, 4 G. Laing(AUS) Norton, 5 L. Simpson(NZ) AJS, 6 M. Quincey(AUS) Norton.

500 cc: 1 R. Amm(Rhod) Norton 87.81 mph, 2 R. Coleman(NZ) AJS, 3 G. Laing(AUS) Norton, 4 M. Quincey (AUS) Norton, 5 J. Surtees(GB) Norton, 6 J. Ahearn(AUS) Norton.

Sidecar: 1 E. Oliver/L. Nutt(GB) Norton 76.41 mph, 2 C. Smith/S. Dibben(GB) Norton, 3 W. Noll/F. Cron(D) BMW, 4 F. Hillebrand/M. Grunwald(D) BMW, 5 W. Schnieder/H. Strauss(D) BMW, 6 J. Drion(F)/I. Stoll(D) Norton.

Dutch TT

125 cc: 1 R. Hollaus(A) NSU, 85.31 mph, 2 H-P Muller (D) NSU, 3 C. Ubbiali(I) MV, 4 H. Baltisberger(D) NSU, 5 W. Haas(D)D NSU, 6 K. Lottes(D) MV.

250 cc: 1 W. Haas(D) NSU 95.40 mph, 2 R. Hollaus(A) NSU, 3 H. Baltisberger(D) NSU, 4 K. Kavanagh(AUS) Guzzi, 5 H-P Muller(D) NSU, 6 A. Wheeler(GB) Guzzi.

350 cc: 1 F. Anderson(GB) Guzzi 97.65 mph, 2 E. Lorenzetti(I) Guzzi, 3 R. Coleman(NZ) AJS, 4 B. McIntyre(GB) AJS, 5 K. Hoffman(D) DKW, 6 A. Montanari(I) Guzzi.

500 cc: 1 G. Duke(GB) Gilera 104.18 mph, 2 F. Anderson (GB) Guzzi, 3 C. Bandirola(I) MV, 4 R. Coleman(NZ) AJS, 5 D. Dale(GB) MV, 6 B. McIntyre(GB) AJS.

German GP

125 cc: 1 R. Hollaus(A) NSU 78.86 mph, 2 W. Haas
(D) NSU, 3 C. Ubbiali(I) MV, 4 H-P Muller(D) NSU,
5 C. Sandford(GB) MV, 6 K. Lottes(D) MV.

250 cc: 1 W. Haas(D) NSU 84,58 mph, 2 R. Hollaus(A)
NSU, 3 R. Hallmeier(D) Adler, 4 A. Wheeler(GB) Guzzi,
5 W. Reichert(D) NSU, 6 W. Vogel(D) Adler.

350 cc: 1 R. Amm(Rhod) Norton, 83.58 mph,
2 R. Coleman(NZ) AJS, 3 J. Brett(GB) Norton, 4 M. Quincey
(AUS) Norton, 5 L. Simpson(NZ) AJS, 6 G. Braun(D) Horex.

500 cc: 1 G. Duke(GB) Gilera 89.48 mph, 2 R. Amm
(Rhod) Norton, 3 R. Armstrong(IRL) Gilera,
4 K. Kavanagh (AUS) Guzzi, 5 F. Anderson(GB) Guzzi,
6 J. Brett(GB) Norton.

Sidecar: 1 W. Noll/F. Cron(D) BMW, 76.25 mph,
2 W. Schneider/H. Strauss(D) BMW, 3 C. Smith/S. Dibben
(GB) Norton, 4 O. Schmid/O. Kolle(D) Norton,
5 L. Neussner/W. Oxner(D) Norton, 6 E. Kussin/F. Steidel
(A) Norton.

Italian GP

125 cc: 1 G. Sala(I) MV 90.99 mph, 2 T. Provini(I)
Mondial, 3 C. Ubbiali(I) MV, 4 M. Genevini(I) MV,
5 F. Bertoni(I) MV, 6 W. Scheidhauer(D) MV.

250 cc: 1 A. Wheeler(GB) Guzzi 92.31 mph, 2 R. Ferri(I)
Guzzi, 3 K. Knopf(D) NSU, 4 R. Colombo(I) Guzzi,
5 T. Wood(GB) Guzzi, 6 A. Marelli(I) Guzzi.

350 cc: 1 F. Anderson(GB) Guzzi 101.63 mph,
2 E. Lorenzetti(I) Guzzi, 3 K. Kavanagh(AUS) Guzzi,
4 D. Agostini(I) Guzzi, 5 R. Amm(Rhod) Norton, 6 J. Brett
(GB) Norton.

500 cco: 1 G. Duke(GB) Gilera 111.45 mph, 2 U. Masetti
(I) Gilera, 3 C. Bandirola(I) MV 4 D. Dale(GB) MV,
5 R. Armstrong(IRL) Gilera, 6 K. Kavanagh(AUS) Guzzi.

Sidecar: 1 W. Noll/F. Cron(D) BMW 93.13 mph,
2 C. Smith/S. Dibben(GB) Norton, 3 W. Faust/K. Remmert
(D) BMW, 4 J. Drion(F)/I. Stoll(D) BMW, 5 F. Hille-
brand/M. Grunwald(D) BMW, 6 R. Betemps/A. Drivet
(F) Norton.

Spanish GP

125 cc: T. Provini(I) Mondial 64.52 mph, 2 R. Colombo
(I) MV, 3 A. Elizade(S) Montesa, 4 J. Bertran(S) Montesa,
5 C. Paragues(S) Lube, 6 V. Corsin(S) MV.

350 cc: 1 F. Anderson(GB) Guzzi 66.42 mph,
2 D. Agostini(I) Guzzi, 3 J. Grace(Gib) Norton, 3 G. Braun
(D) NSU, 5 B. Matthews(GB) Velocette, 6 A. Goffin(B)
Norton.

500 cc: 1 D. Dale(GB) MV 66.90 mph, 2 K. Kavanagh
(AUS) Guzzi, 3 N. Pagani(I) MV, 4 T. Wood(GB) Norton,
5 A. Goffin(B) Norton, 6 J. Clark(GB) Norton.

Swiss GP

250 cc: 1 R. Hollaus(A) NSU 78.82 mph, 2 G. Braun(D)
NSU, 3 H-P Muller(D) NSU, 4 L. Taveri(CH) Guzzi,
5 R. Colombo(I) Guzzi, 6 W. Vogel(D) Adler.

350 cc: 1 F. Anderson(GB) Guzzi 87.84 mph,
2 K. Kavanagh(AUS) Guzzi, 3 R. Amm(Rhod) Norton,
4 J. Brett(GB) Norton, 5 R. Coleman(NZ) AJS,
6 B. McIntyre(GB) AJS.

500 cc: 1 G. Duke(GB) Gilera 93.67 mph, 2 R. Amm(Rhod)
Norton, 3 R. Armstrong(IRL) Gilera, 4 J. Brett(GB)
Norton, 5 R. Coleman(NZ) AJS, 6 D. Farrant(GB) AJS.

Sidecar: 1 W. Noll/F. Cron(D) BMW 80.79 mph,
2 C. Smith/S. Dibben(GB) Norton, 3 W. Faust/K. Remmert
(D) BMW, 4 W. Schneider/H. Strass(D) BMW, 5 E. Oliver/
L. Nutt(GB) Norton, 6 H. Haldemann/L. Taveri(CH)
Norton.

French GP

250 cc: 1 W. Haas(D) NSU 101.02 mph, 2 H-P Muller(D)
NSU, 3 R. Hollaus(A) NSU, 4 H. Baltisberger(D)
NSU, 5 T. Wood(GB) Guzzi, 6 L. Baviera(I) Guzzi.

350 cc: 1 P. Monneret(F) AJS 95.57 mph, 2 A. Goffin(B)
Norton, 3 B. Matthews(GB) Velocette, 4 J. Collot(F)
Norton, 5 C. Stormont(NZ) BSA, 6 F. Dauwe(B) Norton.

500 cc: 1 P. Monneret(F) Gilera 108.62 mph, 2 A. Milani
(I) Gilera, 3 J. Collot(F) Norton, 4 L. Taveri(CH) Norton,
5 B. Matthews(GB) Norton, 6 C. Julian(GB) Norton.

Belgian GP

350 cc: 1 K. Kavanagh(AUS) Guzzi 101.64 mph,
2 F. Anderson(GB) Guzzi, 3 S. Wunsche(D) DKW,
4 E. Lorenzetti(I) Guzzi, 5 L. Simpson(NZ) AJS,
6 B. McIntyre(GB) AJS.

500 cc: 1 G. Duke(GB) Gilera 109.51 mph, 2 K. Kavanagh
(AUS) Guzzi, 3 L. Martin(B) Gilera, 4 B. McIntyre(GB)
AJS, 5 K. Campbell(A) Norton, 6 G. Murphy(NZ)
Matchless.

Sidecar: 1 E. Oliver/L. Nutt(GB) Norton 97.83 mph,
2 W. Noll/F. Cron(D) BMW, 3 C. Smith/S. Dibben(GB)
Norton, 4 F. Hillebrand/M. Grunwald(D) BMW,
5 W. Schneider/H. Strauss(D) BMW, 6 J. Deronne/P.
Leys(B) Norton.

World champions

125 cc: 1 R. Hollaus(A) NSU, 2 C. Ubbiali(I) MV,
3 H-P Muller(D) NSU.

250 cc: 1 W. Haas(D) NSU, 2 R. Hollaus(A) NSU,
3 H-P Muller(D) NSU.

350 cc: 1 F. Anderson(GB) Guzzi, 2 R. Amm(Rhod)
Norton, 3 R. Coleman(NZ) AJS.

500 cc: G. Duke(GB) Gilera, 2 R. Amm(Rhod) Norton,
3 K. Kavanagh(AUS) Norton.

Sidecar: 1 W. Noll(D) BMW, 2 E. Oliver(GB) Norton,
3 C. Smith(GB) Norton.

1955

Spanish GP (Barcelona)

125 cc: 1 L. Taveri(CH) MV 65.37 mph, 2 R. Ferri(I) Mondial, 3 C. Ubbiali(I) MV, 4 G. Lattanzi(I) Mondial, 5 A. Copeta(I) MV, 6 M. Cama(S) Montesa.

500 cc: 1 R. Armstrong(IRL) Gilera 109. 246 mph, 2 C. Bandirola(I) MV, 3 U. Masetti(I) MV, 4 O. Valdinoci(I) Gilera, 5 N. Pagani(I) MV, 6 T. Forconi(I) MV.

Sidecars: 1 W. Faust/K. Remmert(D) BMW 61.45 mph, 2 C. Smith/S. Dibben(GB) Norton, 3 E. Oliver/L. Nutt (GB) Norton, 4 R. Koch/C. Wirth(D) BMW, 5 E. Merlo/ D. Magni(I) Gilera, 6 R. Benz/J. Kuchler(CH) Norton.

French GP (Rheims)

125 cc: 1 C. Ubbiali(I) MV 91.65 mph, 2 L. Taveri(CH) MV, 3 G. Lattanzi(I) Mondial, 4 T. Provini(I) Mondial, 5 A. Copeta(I) MV, 6 R. Ferri(I) Mondial.

350 cc: 1 D. Agostini(I) Guzzi 97.32 mph, 2 D. Dale(GB) Guzzi, 3 R. Colombo(I) Guzzi, 4 A. Goffin(B) Norton, 5 G. Murphy(NZ) AJS, 6 J. Collot(F) Norton.

500 cc: 1 G. Duke(GB) Gilera 111.96 mph, 2 L. Liberati (I) Gilera, 3 R. Armstrong(IRL) Gilera, 4 T. Forconi(I) MV, 5 J. Collot(F) Norton, 6 F. Dauwe(B) Norton.

Isle of Man TT races

125 cc: 1 C. Ubbiali(I) MV 69.62 mph, 2 L. Taveri(CH) MV, 3 G. Lattanzi(I) Mondial, 4 B. Lomas(GB) MV, 5 B. Webster(GB) MV, 5 R. Porter(GB) MV.

250 cc: 1 B. Lomas(GB) MV 71.31 mph, 2 C. Sandford (GB) Guzzi, 3 H-P Muller(D) NSU, 4 A. Wheeler(GB) Guzzi, 5 D. Chadwick(GB) RD Special, 6 B. Webster(GB) Velocette.

350 cc: 1 B. Lomas(GB) Guzzi 92.27 mph, 2 B. McIntyre(GB) Norton, 3 C. Sandford(GB) Guzzi, 4 J. Surtees(GB) Norton, 5 M. Quincey(AUS) Norton, 6 J. Hartle(GB) Norton.

500 cc: 1 G. Duke(GB) Gilera 97.86 mph, 2 R. Armstrong (IRL) Gilera, 3 K. Kavanagh(AUS) Guzzi, 4 J. Brett(GB) Norton, 5 B. McIntyre(GB) Norton, 6 D. Ennett(GB) Matchless.

Sidecar: 1 W. Schneider/H. Struss(D) BMW 69.96 mph, 2 B. Boddice/W. Storr(GB) Norton, 3 P. Harris/R. Campbell(GB) Matchless, 4 J. Beeton/E. Billingham(GB) Norton, 5 F. Taylor/R. Taylor(GB) Norton, 6 E. Walker/ D. Roberts(GB) Norton.

German GP (Nürburgring)

125 cc: 1 C. Ubbiali(I) MV 68.62 mph, 2 L. Taveri(CH) MV, 3 R. Venturi(I) MV, 4 K. Lottes(D) MV, 5 K. Pertrusche(D) IFA, 6 E. Krumpholz(D) IFA.

250 cc: 1 H-P Muller(D) NSU 76.87 mph, 2 W. Brandt (D) NSU, 3 C. Sandford(GB) Guzzi, 4 L. Taveri(CH) MV 5 A. Wheeler(GB) Guzzi, 6 H. Hallmeier(D) NSU.

350 cc: 1 B. Lomas(GB) Guzzi 79.42 mph, 2 A. Hobl(D) DKW, 3 J. Surtees(GB) Norton, 4 C. Sandford(GB) Guzzi, 5 K. Kavanagh(AUS) Guzzi, 6 K. Hoffmann(D) DKW.

500 cc: 1 G. Duke(GB) Gilera 81.29 mph, 2 W. Zeller(D) BMW, 3 C. Bandirola(I) MV, 4 U. Masetti(I) MV, 5 G. Colnago(I) Gilera, 6 J. Ahearn(AUS) Norton.

Sidecar: 1 W. Faust/K. Remmert(D) BMW 72.53 mph, 2 W. Noll/F. Cron(D) BMW, 3 W. Schneider/H. Strauss (D) BMW, 4 J. Drion(F)/I. Stoll(D) Norton, 5 B. Mitchell/ G. Max(AUS) Norton, 6 J. Murit(F)/F. Flahaut(Mar) BMW.

Dutch TT (Assen)

125 cc: 1 C. Ubbiali(I) MV 70.15 mph, 2 R. Venturi(I) MV, 3 R. Grimas(N) Mondial, 4 B. Webster(GB) MV, 5 W. Schneidhauer(D) MV, 6 E. Wunsche(D) MV.

250 cc: 1 L. Taveri(CH) MV 75.80 mph, 2 B. Lomas(GB) MV, 3 U. Masetti(I) MV, 4 H-P Muller(D) NSU, 5 E. Lorenzetti(I) Guzzi, 3 C. Sandford(GB) Guzzi.

350 cc: 1 K. Kavanagh(AUS) Guzzi 78.00 mph, 2 B. Lomas (GB) Guzzi, 3 D. Dale(GB) Guzzi, 4 A. Hobl(D) DKW, 5 K. Hoffman(D) DKW, 6 H. Bartle(D) DKW.

500 cc: 1 G. Duke(GB) Gilera 79.85 mph, 2 R. Armstrong (IRL) Gilera, 3 U. Masetti(I) MV, 4 H. Veer(N) Gilera, 5 B. Brown(AUS) Matchless, 6 E. Grant(NZ) Norton.

Sidecar: 1 W. Faust/K. Remmert(D) BMW 72.08 mph, 2 W. Noll/F. Cron(D) BMW, 3 B. Mitchell/G. Max(A) Norton, 4 J. Murit/F. Flahaut(Mar) BMW, 5 J. Drion(F)/ I. Stoll(D) Norton, 6 H. Steman/M. Dahaas(N) BMW.

Italian GP (Monza)

125 cc: 1 C. Ubbiali(I) MV 93.91 mph, 2 R. Venturi(I) MV, 3 A. Copeta(I) MV, 4 A. Hobl(D) DKW, 5 S. Wunsche(D) DKW, 6 P. Campanelli(I) Mondial.

250 cc: 1 C. Ubbiali(I) MV 101.21 mph, 2 H. Baltisberger (D) NSU, 3 S. Miller(GB) NSU, 4 H-P Muller(D) NSU, 5 B. Lomas(GB) MV, 6 U. Masetti(I) MV.

350 cc: 1 D. Dale(GB) Guzzi 104.50 mph, 2 B. Lomas(GB) Guzzi, 3 K. Kavanagh(AUS) Guzzi, 4 E. Lorenzetti(I) Guzzi, 5 A. Hobl(D) DKW, 6 R. Columbo(I) Guzzi.

500 cc: 1 U. Masetti(I) MV 110.15 mph, 2 R. Armstrong (IRL) Gilera, 3 G. Duke(GB) Gilera, 4 G. Colnago(I) Gilera, 5 A. Milani(I) Gilera, 6 E. Riedelbauch(D) BMW.

Sidecar: 1 W. Noll/F. Cron(D) BMW 93.23 mph, 2 W. Schneider/H. Strauss(D) BMW, 3 J Drion(F)/I. Stoll (D) Norton, 4 F. Camathias/M. Bula(CH) BMW, 5 J. Murit (F)/ F. Flahaut(Mar) BMW, 6 F. Seeber/F. Heiss(D) BMW.

Ulster GP

250 cc: 1 J. Surtees(GB) NSU 87.57 mph, 2 S. Miller(GB) NSU, 3 U. Masetti(I) MV, 4 B. Lomas(GB) MV, 5 C. Sandford(GB) Guzzi, 6 H-P Muller(D) NSU.

350 cc: 1 B. Lomas(GB) Guzzi 89.25 mph, 2 J. Hartle(GB) Norton, 3 J. Surtees(GB) Norton, 4 C. Sandford(GB) Guzzi, 5 B. McIntyre(GB) Norton, 6 G. Murphy(NZ) AJS.

1956

500 cc: 1 B. Lomas(GB) Guzzi 92.22 mph, 2 J. Hartle(GB) Norton, 3 D. Dale(GB) Guzzi, 4 B. McIntyre(GB) Norton, 5 G. Murphy(NZ) Matchless, 6 J. Clark(GB) Matchless.

Belgian GP (Spa)

350 cc: 1 B. Lomas(GB) Guzzi 105.61 mph, 2 A. Hobl(D) DKW, 3 K. Campbell(AUS) Norton, 4 C Sandford(GB) Guzzi, 5 R. Colombo(I) Guzzi, 6 H. Bartle(D) DKW.

500 cc: 1 G. Colnago(I) Gilera 111.17 mph, 2 P. Monneret (F) Gilera, 3 L. Martin(B) Gilera, 4 D. Agostini(I) Guzzi, 5 A Goffin(B) Norton, 6 J. Storr(GB) Norton.

Sidecar: 1 W. Noll/F. Cron(D) BMW 96.02 mph, 2 W. Faust/K. Remmert(D) BMW, 3 W. Schneider/H. Strauss (D) BMW, 4 J. Deronne/P. Leys(B) BMW, 5 P. Harris/ R. Campbell(GB) Matchless, 6 J. Drion(F)/I. Stoll(D) Norton.

World champions

125 cc: 1 C. Ubbiali(I) MV, 2 L. Taveri(CH) MV, 3 R. Venturi(I) MV.

250 cc: H-P Muller(D) NSU, 2 C. Sandford(GB) Guzzi, 3 W. Lomas(GB) MV.

350 cs: 1 W. Lomas(GB) Guzzi, 2 D. Dale(GB) Guzzi, 3 A. Hobl(D) DKW.

500 cc: 1 G. Duke(GB) Gilera, 2 R. Armstrong(IRL) Gilera, 3 U. Masetti(I) MV.

Sidecar: 1 W. Faust(D) BMW, 2 W. Noll(D) BMW, 3 W. Schneider(D) BMW.

Isle of Man TT races

125 cc: 1 C. Ubbiali(I) Mv 69.73 mph, 2 M. Cama(S) Montesa, 3 F. Gonzales(S) Montesa, 4 E. Sirera(S) Montesa, 5 D. Chadwick(GB) LEF, 6 V. Parus(CZ) CZ.

250 cc: 1 C. Ubbiali(I) MV 67.00 mph, 2 R. Colombo(I) MV, 3 H. Baltisberger(D) NSU, 4 H. Kassner(D) NSU, 5 F. Bartos(C) CZ, 6 A. Wheeler(GB) Guzzi.

350 cc: 1 K. Kavanagh(AUS) Guzzi 89.26 mph, 2 D. Ennett (GB) AJS, 3 J. Hartle(GB) Norton, 4 C. Sandford(GB) DKW, 5 E. Grant(SA) Norton, 6 A. Trow(GB) Norton.

500 cc: 1 J. Surtees(GB) MV 96.50 mph, 2 J. Hartle(GB) Norton, 3 J. Brett(GB) Norton, 4 W. Zeller(D) BMW, 5 B. Lomas(GB) Guzzi, 6 D. Ennett(GB) Matchless.

Sidecar: 1 F. Hillebrand/M. Grunwald(D) BMW 69.64 mph, 2 P. Harris/R. Campbell(GB) Norton, 3 B. Boddice/ W. Storr(GB) Norton, 4 B. Mitchell(AUS)/E. Bliss(GB) Norton, 5 J. Beeton/L. Nutt(GB) Norton, 6 E. Walker/ D. Roberts(GB) Norton.

Dutch TT (Assen)

125 cc: C. Ubbiali(I) MV 74.88 mph, 2 L. Taveri(CH) MV, 3 A. Hobl(D) DKW, 4 C. Sandford(GB) Mondial, 5 K. Hoffman(D) DKW, 6 F. Bartos(CZ) CZ.

250 cc: 1 C. Ubbiali(I) MV 78.15 mph, 2 L. Taveri(CH) MV, 3 E. Lorenzetti(I) Guzzi, 4 R. Colombo(I) MV, 5 H. Kassner(D) NSU, 6 J. Kostir(CZ) CZ.

350 cc: 1 B. Lomas(GB) Guzzi 80.48 mph, 2 J. Surtees (GB) MV, 3 A. Hobl(D) DKW, 4 C. Sandford(GB) DKW, 5 K. Kavanagh(AUS) Guzzi, 6 D. Dale(GB) Guzzi.

500 cc: 1 J. Surtees(GB) MV 82.40 mph, 2 W. Zeller(D) BMW, 3 E. Grant(SA) Norton, 4 K. Bryen(AUS) Norton, 5 P. Fahey(NZ) Matchless, 6 E. Hiller(D) BMW.

Sidecar: 1 F. Hillebrand/M. Grunwald(D) BMW 73.37 mph, 2 W. Noll/F. Cron(D) BMW, 3 C. Smith/ S. Dibben(GB) Norton, 4 B. Mitchell(AUS)/E. Bliss(GB) Norton, 5 F. Camathias/M. Bula(CH) BMW, 6 J. Drion (F)/I. Stoll(D) BMW.

Belgian GP (Spa)

125 cc: 1 C. Ubbiali(I) MV 99.85 mph, 2 F. Libanon(I) MV, 3 P. Monneret(F) Gilera, 4 L. Taveri(CH) MV, 5 K. Hoffmann(D) DKW, 6 J. Grace(GIB) Montesa.

250 cc: 1 C. Ubbiali(I) MV 104.76 mph, 2 L. Taveri(CH) MV, 3 H. Kassner(D) NSU, 4 K. Koster(N) NSU, 5 L. Simons(NL) NSU, 6 J-P Bayle(F) NSU.

350 cc: 1 J. Surtees(GB) MV 109.58 mph, 2 A. Hobl(D) DKW, 3 C. Sandford(GB) DKW, 4 K. Hoffmann(D) DKW, 5 U. Masetti(I) MV, 6 H. Bartl(D) DKW.

500 cc: 1 J. Surtees(GB) MV 114.31 mph, 2 W. Zeller(D) BMW, 3 P. Monneret(F) Gilera, 4 U. Masetti(I) MV, 5 A. Milani(I) Gilera, 6 A. Goffin(B) Norton.

Sidecar: 1 W. Noll/F. Cron(D) BMW 97.22 mph, 2 P. Harris/R. Campbell(GB) Norton, 3 B. Mitchell(AUS)/ E. Bliss(GB) Norton, 4 F. Hillebrand/M. Grunwad(D) BMW, 5 H. Fath/E. Ohr(D) BMW, 6 J. Drion(F)/ I. Stoll(D) BMW.

German GP (Solitude)

125 cc: 1 R. Ferri(I) Gilera 84.94 mph, 2 C. Ubbiali(I) MV, 3 T. Provini(I) Mondial, 4 F. Libanon(I) MV, 5 A. Hobl(D) DKW, 6 K. Hoffmann(D) DKW.

250 cc: 1 C. Ubbiali(I) MV 87.81 mph, 2 L. Taveri(CH) MV, 3 R. Venturi(I) MV, 4 H. Baltisberger(D) NSU, 5 B. Brown(AUS) NSU, 6 R. Heck(D) NSU.

350 cc: 1 B. Lomas(GB) Guzzi 90.79 mph, 2 A. Hobl(D) DKW, 3 D. Dale(GB) Guzzi, 4 C. Sandford(GB) DKW, 5 H. Bartl(D) DKW, 6 B. Matthews(GB) Norton.

500 cc: 1 R. Armstrong(IRL) Gilera 92.34 mph, 2 U. Masetti(I) MV, 3 P. Monneret(F) Gilera, 4 G. Klinger (A) BMW, 5 E. Grant(SA) Norton, 6 K. Bryen(AUS) Norton.

Sidecar: 1 W. Noll/F. Cron(D) BMW 84.95 mph, 2 F. Hillebrand/M. Grunwald(D) BMW, 3 H. Fath/E. Ohr (D) BMW, 4 W. Schneider/H. Strauss(D) BMW, 5 C. Smith/ S. Dibben(GB) Norton, 6 L. Neussner/D. Hess(D) BMW.

Ulster GP

125 cc: 1 C. Ubbiali(I) MV 80.94 mph, 2 R. Ferri(I) Gilera, 3 B. Webster(GB) MV, 4 C. Maddrick(GB) MV, 5 E. Cope(GB) MV Five finishers only.

250 cc: 1 L. Taveri(CH) MV 86.28 mph, 2 S. Miller(GB) NSU, 3 A. Wheeler(GB) Guzzi, 4 B. Coleman(NZ) NSU, 5 C. Maddrick(GB) Guzzi, 6 M. Bula(CH) NSU.

350 cc: 1 B. Lomas(GB) Guzzi 89.98 mph, 2 D. Dale(GB) Guzzi, 3. J. Hartle(GB) Norton, 4 J. Brett(GB) Norton, 5 G. Murphy(NZ) AJS, 6 B. Brown(AUS) AJS.

500 cc: 1 J. Hartle(GB) Norton 85.61 mph, 2 B. Brown(AUS) Matchless, 3 G. Murphy(NZ) Matchless, 4 G. Tanner(GB) Norton, 5 R. Herron(GB) Norton, 6 J. Brett(GB) Norton.

Sidecar: 1 W. Noll/F. Cron(D) BMW 78.82 mph, 2 P. Harris/R. Campbell(GB) Norton, 3 F. Camathias/ M. Bula(CH) BMW, 4 F. Taylor(GB) Norton, 5 B. Beevers/ J. Mundy(GB) Norton, 6 J. Winjs(B)/M. Woollett(GB) BMW.

Italian GP

125 cc: C. Ubbiali(I) MV 99.81 mph, 2 T. Provini(I) Mondial, 3 R. Sartori(I) Mondial, 4 L. Taveri(CH) MV, 5 S. Artusi(I) Ducati, 6 K Hoffmann(D) DKW.

250 cc: 1 C. Ubbiali(I) MV 103.71 mph, 2 E. Lorenzetti(I) Guzzi, 3 R. Venturi(I) MV, 4 L. Taveri(CH) MV, 5 A. Montanari(I) Guzzi, 6 S. Miller(GB) NSU.

350 cc: 1 L. Liberati(I) Gilera 110.78 mph, 2 D. Dale(GB) Guzzi, 3 R. Colombo(I) MV, 4 K. Hoffmann(D) DKW, 5 C. Sandford(GB) DKW, 6 A. Hobl(D) DKW.

500 cc: 1 G. Duke(GB) Gilera 113.59 mph, 2 L. Liberati (I) Gilera, 3 P. Monneret(F) Gilera, 4 R. Armstrong(GB) Gilera, 5 C. Bandirola(I) MV, 6 W. Zeller(D) BMW.

Sidecar: 1 A. Milani/R. Milani(I) Gilera 97.68 mph, 2 P. Harris/R. Campbell(GB) Norton, 3 F. Hillebrand/M. Grunwäld(D) BMW, 4 F. Camathias/M. Bula(CH) BMW, 5 J. Drion(F)/I. Stoll(D) BMW, 6 W. Schneider/ H. Strauss(D) BMW.

World champions

125 cc: 1 C. Ubbiali(I) MV, 2 R. Ferri(I) Gilera, 3 L. Taveri(CH) MV.

250 cc: 1 C. Ubbiali(I) MV, 2 L. Taveri(CH) MV, 3 E. Lorenzetti(I) Guzzi.

350 cc: 1 W. Lomas(GB) Guzzi, 2 A. Hobl(D) DKW, 3 J. Hartle(GB) Norton.

500 cc: J. Surtees(GB) MV, 2 W. Zeller(D) BMW, 3 J. Hartle(GB) Norton.

Sidecars: 1 W. Noll(D) BMW, 2 F. Hillebrand(D) BMW, 3 P. Harris(GB) Norton.

1957

German GP (Hockenheim)

125 cc: 1 C. Ubbiali(I) MV 99.23 mph, 2 T. Provini(I) Mondial, 3 R. Colombo(I) MV, 4 H. Fugner(D) MZ, 5 L. Taveri(CH) MV, 6 E. Degner(D) MZ.

250 cc 1 C. Ubbiali(I) MV 109.79 mph, 2 R. Colombo(I) MV, 3 C. Sandford(GB) Mondial, 4 E. Lorenzetti(I) Guzzi, 5 L. Taveri(CH) MV, 6 H. Hallmeier(D) NSU.

350 cc: 1 L. Liberati(I) Gilera 106.74 mph, 2 J. Hartle(GB) Norton, 3 H. Hallmeier(D) NSU, 4 U. Masetti(I) MV, 5 A*i* Montanari(I) Guzzi, 6 R. Thompson(AUS) AJS.

500 cc: 1 L. Liberati(I) Gilera 124.20 mph, 2 B. McIntyre(GB) Gilera, 3 W. Zeller(D) BMW, 4 D. Dale (GB) Guzzi, 5 T. Shepherd(GB) MV, 6 E. Hiller(D) BMW

Sidecar: 1 F. Hillebrand/M. Grunwald(D) BMW 101.84 mph, 2 W. Schneider/H. Strauss(D) BMW, 3 J. Knebel/ R. Amfaldern(D) BMW, 4 F. Camathias/J. Galliker(CH) BMW, 5 L. Neussner/D. Hess(D) BMW.

Isle of Man TT races

125 cc: 1 T. Provini(I) Mondial 73.61 mph, 2 C. Ubbiali(I) MV, 3 L. Taveri(CH) MV, 4 S. Miller(GB) Mondial, 5 C. Sandford(GB) Mondial, 6 R. Colombo(I) MV.

250 cc: 1 C. Sandford(GB) Mondial 75.73 mph, 2 L. Taveri(CH) MV, 3 R. Colombo(I) MV, 4 F. Bartos (CZ) CZ, 5 S. Miller(GB) Mondial, 6 D. Chadwick(GB) MV.

350 cc: 1 B. McIntyre(GB) Gilera 94.91 mph, 2 K. Campbell(AUS) Guzzi, 3 B. Brown(AUS) Gilera, 4 J. Surtees(GB) MV, 5 E. Hinton(AUS) Norton, 6 G. Murphy(NZ) AJS.

500 cc: 1 B. McIntyre(GB) Gilera 98.93 mph, 2 J. Surtees (GB) MV, 3 B. Brown(AUS) Gilera, 4 D. Dale(GB) Guzzi, 5 K. Campbell(AUS) Guzzi, 6 A. Trow(GB) Norton.

Sidecar: 1 F. Hillebrand/M. Grunwald(D) BMW 71.84 mph, 2 W. Schneider/H. Strauss(D) BMW, 3 F. Camathias/J. Galliker(CH) BMW, 4 J. Beeton/ C. Billingham(GB(Norton, 5 C. Freeman/J. Chisnell(GB) Norton, 6 P. Woollett/G. Loft(GB) Norton.

Dutch TT (Assen)

125 cc: 1 T. Provini(I) Mondial 76.68 mph, 2 R. Colombo (I) MV, 3 L. Taveri(CH) MV, 4 C. Sanderford(GB) Mondial, 5 F. Libanon(I) MV, 6 S. Miller(GB) Mondial.

250 cc: 1 T. Provini(I) Mondial 79.50 mph, 2 C. Sandford (GB) Mondial, 3 S. Miller(GB) Mondial, 4 F. Libanon (GB) MV, 5 F. Stastny(CZ) Jawa, 6 A. Wheeler(GB) Guzzi.

350 cc: 1 K. Campbell(AUS) Guzzi 82.28 mph, 2 B. McIntyre (GB) Gilera, 3 L. Liberati(I) Gilera, 4 J. Brett(GB) Norton, 5 K. Bryen(AUS) Norton, 6 J. Hartle(GB) Norton.

500 cc: 1 J. Surtees(GB) MV 82.47 mph, 2 L. Liberati(I) Gilera, 3 W. Zeller(D) BMW, 4 J. Brett(GB) Norton, 5 E. Hiller(D) BMW, 6 K. Bryen(AUS) Norton.

Sidecar: 1 F. Hillebrand/M. Grunwald(D) BMW 72.94 mph, 2 J. Beeton/T. Partige(GB) Norton, 3 L. Neussner/ D. Hess(D) BMW, 4 E. Strub(CH)/H. Cecco(D) BMW, 5 M. Beauvais/A. Coudert(F) Norton, 6 M. Grossmann/ W. Volk(D) Norton.

Belgian GP (Spa)

125 cc: 1 T. Provini(I) Mondial 102.16 mph, 2 L. Taveri (CH) MV, 3 C. Sandford(GB) Mondial, 4 F. Bartos(CZ) CZ, 5 B. Webster(GB) MV, 6 C. Meddrick(GB) MV.

250 cc: 1 J. Hartle(GB) MV 106.51 mph, 2 S. Miller(GB) Mondial, 3 C. Sandford(GB) Mondial, 4 A. Wheeler(GB) Guzzi, 5 F. Bartos(CZ) CZ, 5 G. Beer(D) Adler.

350 cc: 1 K. Campbell(AUS) Guzzi 114.26 mph, 2 L. Liberati (I) Gilera, 3 K. Bryen(AUS) Guzzi, 4 A. Montanari(I) Guzzi, 5 B. Brown(AUS) Gilera, 6 G. Colnagao(I) Guzzi.

500 cc: 1 J. Brett(GB) Norton 113.35 mph, 2 K. Bryen(AUS) Norton, 3 D. Minter(GB) Norton, 4 M. O'Rourke(GB) Norton, 5 H. Jaeger(D) BMW. Five finishers only.

Sidecar: 1 W. Scheider/H. Strauss(D) BMW, 2 F. Camathias/J. Galliker(CH) BMW, 3 F. Hillebrand/M. Grunwald(D) BMW, 4 P. Harris/R. Campbell(GB) Norton, 5 J. Drion(F)/I. Stoll(D) BMW, 6 M. Beauvais/ A. Coudert(F) Norton.

Ulster GP

125 cc: 1 L. Taveri(CH) MV 78.26 mph, 2 T. Provini(I) Mondial, 3 R. Venturi(I) MV, 4 D. Chadwick(GB) MV 5 S. Miller(GB) Mondial, 6 B. Webster(GB) MV.

250 cc: 1 C. Sandford(GB) Mondial 85.21 mph, 2 D. Chadwick(GB) MV, 3 T. Robb(GB) NSU, 4 B. Brown (AUS) NSU, 5 G. Andrews(GB) NSU, 6 L. Hodgins(GB) Velocette.

359 cc: 1 K. Campbell(AUS) Guzzi 85.21 mph, 2 K. Bryen (AUS) Guzzi, 3 L. Liberati(I) Gilera, 4 J. Hartle(GB) Norton, 5 D. Chadwick(GB) Norton, 6 F. Purslow(GB) Norton.

500 cc: 1 L. Liberati(I) Gilera 91.48 mph, 2 B. McIntyre (GB) Gilera, 3 G. Duke(GB) Gilera, 4 G. Tanner(GB) Norton, 5 K. Bryen(AUS) Guzzi, 6 T. Shepherd(GB) MV.

Italian GP (Monza)

125 cc: 1 C. Ubbiali(I) MV 99.13 mph, 2 S. Miller(GB) Mondial, 3 L. Taveri(CH) MV, 4 F. Libanon(I) MV, 5 R. Venturi(I) MV, 6 G. Sala(I) Mondial.

250 cc: 1 T. Provini(I) Mondial 109.36 mph, 2 R. Venturi(I) MV, 3 E. Lorenzetti(I) Guzzi, 4 C. Sandford (GB) Mondial, 5 S. Miller(GB) Mondial, 6 A. Montanari (I) Guzzi.

350 cc: 1 B. McIntyre(GB) Gilera 111.81 mph, 2 G. Colnago(I) Guzzi, 3 L. Liberati(I) Gilera, 4 A. Milani(I) Gilera, 5 A. Mandolini(I) Guzzi, 6 J. Hartle(GB) Norton.

500 cc: 1. L. Liberati(I) Gilera 115.67 mph, 2 G. Duke (GB) Gilera, 3 A. Milani(I) Gilera, 4 J. Surtees(GB) MV, 5 U. Masetti(I) MV, 6 T. Shepherd(GB) MV.

Sidecar: 1 A. Milani/R. Milani(I) Gilera 99.02 mph, 2 C. Smith/E. Bliss(GB) Norton, 3 F. Camathias(CH)/ H. Cecco(D) BMW, 4 F. Scheidegger(CH)/H. Burckhardt (D) BMW, 5 J. Drion(F)/I. Stoll(D) BMW, 6 L. Neussner/ D. Hess(D) BMW.

World champions

125 cc: 1 T. Provini(I) Mondial, 2 L. Taveri(CH) MV, 3 C. Ubbiali(I) MV.

250 cc: 1 C. Sandford(GB) Mondial, 2 T. Provini(I) Mondial, 3 S. Miller(GB) Mondial.

350 cc: 1 K. Campbell(A) Guzzi, 2 B. McIntyre(GB) Gilera, 3 L. Liberati(I) Gilera.

500 cc: 1 L. Liberati(I) Gilera, 2 B. McIntyre(GB) Gilera, 3 J. Surtees(GB) MV.

Sidecar: 1 F. Hillebrand(D) BMW, 2 W. Schneider(D) BMW, 3 F. Camathias(CH) BMW.

Isle of Man TT races

125 cc: 1 C. Ubbiali(I) MV 72.81 mph, 2 R. Ferri(I) Ducati, 3 D. Chadwick(GB) Ducati, 4 S. Miller(GB) Ducati, 5 E. Degner(D) MZ, 6 H. Fugner(D) MZ.

250 cc: 1 T. Provini(I) MV 76.84 mph, 2 C. Ubbiali(I) MV, 3 M. Hailwood(GB) NSU, 4 B. Brown(AUS) NSU, 5 D Falk(D) Adler, 6 S. Miller(GB) Ducati.

350 cc: 1 J. Surtees(GB) MV 93.91 mph, 2 D. Chadwick (GB) Norton, 3 G. Tanner(GB) Norton, 4 T. Shepherd (GB) Norton, 5 G. Catlin(GB) Norton, 6 A. King(GB) Norton.

500 cc: 1 J. Surtees(GB) MV 98.52 mph, 2 B. Anderson (GB) Norton, 3 B. Brown(AUS) Norton, 4 D. Minter(GB) Norton, 5 D. Chadwick(GB) Norton, 6 H. Anderson(NZ) Norton.

Sidecar: 1 W. Schneider/H. Strauss(D) BMW 72.96 mph, 2 F. Camathias(CH)/H. Cecco(D) BMW, 3 J. Beeton/E. Bulgin(GB) Norton, 4 A. Ritter/F. Blauth(D) BMW, 5 R. Walker/ D. Roberts(GB) Norton, 6 P. Woollett/G. Loft (GB) Norton.

Belgian GP (Spa)

125 cc: 1 A. Gandossi(I) Ducati 98.03 mph 2 R. Ferri(I) Ducati, 3 T. Provini(I) MV, 4 D. Chadwick(GB) Ducati, 5 C. Ubbiali(I) MV, 6 L. Taveri(CH) Ducati.

350 cc: 1 J. Surtees(GB) MV 110.41 mph, 2 J. Hartle(GB) MV, 3 K. Campbell(AUS) Norton, 4 D. Minter(GB) Norton, 5 G. Duke(GB) Norton, 6 D. Chadwick(GB) Norton.

500 cc: 1 J. Surtees(GB) MV 115.25 mph, 2 K. Campbell (AUS) Norton, 3 J. Hartle(GB) MV, 4 G. Duke(GB) BMW, 5 D. Dale(GB) BMW, 6 B. Anderson(GB) Norton.

Sidecar: 1 W. Schneider/H. Strauss(D) BMW 102.99 mph, 2 F. Camathias(CH)/H. Cecco(D) BMW, 3 H. Fath/ F. Rudolf(D) BMW, 4 C. Smith/S. Dibben(GB) Norton, 5 J. Beeton/E. Bulgin(GB) Norton, 6 L. Neussner/D. Hess (D) BMW.

Dutch TT (Assen)

125 cc: 1 C. Ubbiali(I) MV 77.48 mph, 2 L. Taveri(CH) Ducati, 3 T. Provini(I) MV, 4 A. Gandossi(I) Ducati, 5 D. Chadwick(GB) Ducati, 6 E. Degner(D) MZ.

250 cc: 1 T. Provini(I) MV 77.85 mph, 2 C. Ubbiali(I) MV, 3 D. Falk(D) Adler, 4 M. Hailwood(GB) NSU, 5 A. Wheeler(GB) Mondial, 6 H. Kassner(D) NSU.

350 cc: 1 J. Surtees(GB) MV 81.37 mph, 2 J. Hartle(GB) MV, 3 K. Campbell(AUS) Norton, 4 D. Minter(GB) Norton, 5 M. Hailwood(GB) Norton, 6 L. Taveri(CH) Norton.

500 cc: 1 J. Surtees(GB) MV 83.80 mph, 2 J. Hartle(GB) MV, 3 D. Minter(GB) Norton, 4 E. Hiller(D) BMW, 5 D. Dale(GB) BMW, 6 G. Hocking(Rhod) Norton.

Sidecar: 1 F. Camathias(CH)/H. Cecco(D) BMW 74.32 mph, 2 W. Schneider/H. Strauss(D) BMW, 3 H. Fath/ F. Rudolf(D) BMW, 4 C. Smith/S. Dibben(GB) Norton, 5 B. Boddice/B. Canning(GB) Norton, 6 L. Neussner/ D. Hess(D) BMW.

1958

German GP (Nürburgring)

125 cc: 1 C. Ubbiali(I) MV 75.63 mph, 2 T. Provini(I) MV, 3 E. Degner(D) MZ, 4 H. Fugner(D) MZ, 5 W. Brehme(D) MZ, 6 W. Musiol(D) MZ.

250 cc: 1 T. Provini(I) MV 77.89 mph, 2 H. Fugner(D) MZ, 3 D. Falk(D) Adler, 4 H. Kassner(D) NSU, 5 X. Heiss(D) NSU, 6 W. Reichert(D) NSU.

350 cc: 1 J. Surtees(GB) MV 80.41 mph, 2 J. Hartle(GB) MV, 3 D. Chadwick(GB) Norton, 4 M. Hailwood(GB) Norton, 5 B. Anderson(GB) Norton, 6 D. Dale(GB) Norton.

500 cc: 1 J. Surtees(GB) MV 69.92 mph, 2 J. Hartle(GB) MV, 3 G. Hocking (Rhod) Norton, 4 E. Hiller(D) BMW, 5 D. Dale(GB) BMW, 6 B. Brown(AUS) Norton.

Sidecar: 1 W. Schneider/H. Strauss(D) BMW 70.04 mph, 2 F. Camathias(CH)/H. Cecco(D) BMW, 3 R. Richert/ G. Klim(D) BMW, 4 A. Rohsiepe/A. Gardyanczik(D) BMW, 5 L. Neussner/D. Hess(D) BMW, 6 A. Butscher/ H. Munz(D) BMW.

Swedish GP (Hedemora)

125 cc: 1 A. Gandossi(I) Ducati 91.22 mph, 2 L. Taveri (CH) Ducati, 3 C. Ubbiali(I) MV, 4 T. Provini(I) MV, 5 E. Degner(D) MZ, 6 H. Fugner(D) NZ.

250 cc: 1 H. Fugner(D) MZ 94.08 mph, 2 M. Hailwood (GB) NSU, 3 G. Monty(GB) NSU, 4 G. Beer(D) Adler, 5 J. Autengruber(A) NSU, 6 W. Lecke(D) DKW.

350 cc: 1 G. Duke(GB) Norton 97.21 mph, 2 B. Anderson (GB) Norton, 3 M. Hailwood(GB) Norton, 4 A. Trow(GB) Norton, 5 G. Monty(GB) Norton, 6 M. O'Rourke(GB) Norton.

500 cc: 1 G. Duke(GB) Norton 102.65 mph, 2 D. Dale (GB) BMW, 3 T. Shepherd(GB) Norton, 4 G. Hocking (Rhod) Norton, 5 E. Hiller(D) BMW, 6 B. Brown(AUS) Norton.

Ulster GP

125 cc: 1 C. Ubbiali(I) MV u6.97 mph, 2 L. Taveri(CH) Ducati, 3 L. Chadwick(GB) Ducati, 4 A. Gandossi(I) Ducati, 5 H. Fugner(D) MZ, 6 A. Wheeler(GB) Mondial.

250 cc: 1 T. Provini(I) MV 77.34 mph, 2 T. Robb(GB) NSU, 3 D. Chadwick(GB) MV, 4 E. Degner(D) MZ, 5 H. Fugner(D) MZ, 6 D. Dale(GB) NSU.

350 cc: 1 J. Surtees(GB) MV 80.39 mph, 2 J. Hartle(GB) MV, 3 T. Shepherd(GB) Norton, 4 G. Duke(GB) Norton, 5 B. McIntyre(GB) Norton, 6 D. Minter(GB) Norton.

500 cc: 1 J. Surtees(GB) 86.67 mph, 2 B. McIntyre(GB) Norton, 3 J. Hartle(GB) MV, 4 D. Minter(GB) Norton, 5 G. Duke(GB) Norton, 6 D. Dale(GB) BMW.

Italian GP (Monza)

125 cc: 1 B. Spaggiari(I) Ducati 96.76 mph, 2 A. Gandossi (I) Ducati, 3 F. Villa(I) Ducati, 4 D. Chadwick(GB) Ducati, 5 L. Taveri(CH) Ducati, 6 A. Vezzalini(I) MV.

250 cc: 1 E. Mendogni(I) Morini 104.45 mph, 2 G. Zubani(I) Morini, 3 C. Ubbiali(I) MV, 4 G. Beer(D) Adler, 5 J. Autengruber(A) NSU, 6 D. Falk(D) Adler.

350 cc: 1 J. Surtees(GB) MV 107.59 mph, 2 J. Hartle(GB) MV, 3 G. Duke(GB) Norton, 4 B. Anderson(GB) Norton, 5 D. Chadwick(GB) Norton, 6 B. Brown(AUS) AJS.

500 cc: 1 J. Surtees(GB) MV 114.44 mph, 2 R. Venturi(I) MV, 3 U. Masetti(I) MV, 4 D. Dale(GB) BMW, 5 C. Bandirola(I) MV, 6 D. Chadwick(GB) Norton.

World champions

125 cc: 1 C. Ubbiali(I) MV, 2 A. Gandossi(I) Ducati, 3 L. Taveri(CH) Ducati.

250 cc: 1 T. Provini(I) MV. 2 H. Fugner(D) MZ, 3 C. Ubbiali(I) MV.

350 cc: 1 J. Surtees(GB) MV, 2 J. Hartle(GB) MV, 3 G. Duke(GB) Norton.

500 cc: 1 J. Surtees(GB) MV, 2 J. Hartle(GB) MV, 3 D. Dale(GB) BMW.

Sidecar: 1 W. Schneider(D) BMW, 2 F. Camathias(CH) BMW, 3 H. Fath(D) BMW.

1959

Isle of Man TT races

125 cc: 1 T. Provini(I) MV 74.01 mph, 2 L. Taveri(CH) MZ, 3 M. Hailwood(GB) Ducati, 4 H. Fuegner(D) MZ, 5 C. Ubbiali(I) MV, 6 N. Taniguchi(JAP) Honda.

250 cc: 1 T. Provini(I) MV 77.78 mph, 2 C. Ubbiali(I) MV, 3 D. Chadwick(GB) MV, 4 T. Robb(GB) BMS, 5 H. Kassner(D) NSU, 6 R. Thalhammer(A) NSU.

350 cc: 1 J. Surtees(GB) MV 95.34 mph, 2 J. Hartle(GB) MV, 3 A. King(GB) Norton, 4 G. Duke(GB) Norton, 5 B. Anderson(GB) Norton, 6 D. Chadwick(GB) Norton.

500 cc: 1 J. Surtees(GB) MV 87.87 mph, 2 A. King(GB) Norton, 3 B. Brown(AUS) Norton, 4 D. Powell(GB) Matchless, 5 B. McIntyre(GB) Norton, 6 P. Driver(SA) Norton.

Sidecar: 1 W. Schneider(H. Strauss(D) BMW, 72.45 mph, 2 F. Camathias(CH)/H. Cecco(D) BMW, 3 F. Scheidegger (CH)/H. Burckhardt(D) BMW, 4 H. Fath/A. Wohlgemuth (D) BMW, 5 E. Strub/J. Siffert(CH) BMW, 6 O. Greenwood/T. Fairbrother(GB) Triumph.

German GP (Hockenheim)

125 cc: 1 C. Ubbiali(I) MV 97.74 mph, 2 T. Provini(I) MV, 3 M. Hailwood(GB) Ducati, 4 F. Villa(I) Ducati, 5 B. Spaggiari(I) Ducati, 6 E. Degner(D) MZ.

250 cc: 1 C. Ubbiali(I) MV 109.64 mph, 2 E. Mendogni(I) Morini, 3 H. Fuegner(D) MZ, 4 L. Liberati(I) Morini, 5 M. Hailwood(GB) Mondial, 6 G. Duke(GB) Benelli.

350 cc: 1 J. Surtees(GB) MV 110.28 mph, 2 G. Hocking (Rhod) Norton, 3 E. Brambilla(I) MV, 4 G. Duke(GB) Norton, 5 J. Hempleman(NZ) Norton, 6 J. Redman(Rhod) Norton.

500 cc: 1 J. Surtees(GB) MV 123.45 mph, 2 R. Venturi(I) MV, 3 B. Brown(AUS) Norton, 4 K. Kavanagh(AUS) Norton, 5 J. Hempleman(NZ) Norton, 5 A. Huber(D) BMW.

Sidecar: 1 F. Camathias(CH)/H. Cecco(D) BMW 104.96 mph, 2 W. Schneider(H. Strauss(D) BMW, 3 M. Deubel/H. Holer(D) BMW, 4 L. Neussner(D)/ T. Partige(GB) BMW, 5 F. Scheidegger(CH)/H. Burckhardt(D) BMW, 6 A. Rohsiepe/A. Gardyanczik(D) BMW.

Dutch TT (Assen)

125 cc: 1 C. Ubbiali(I) MV 76.64 mph, 2 B. Spaggiari(I) Ducati, 3 M. Hailwood(GB) Ducati, 4 H. Fugner(D) MZ, 5 D. Minter(GB) MZ, 6 K. Kavanagh(AUS) MZ.

250 cc: 1 T. Provini(I) MV 81.62 mph, 2 C. Ubbiali(I) MV, 3 D. Minter(GB) Morini, 4 M. Hailwood(GB) Mondial, 5 H. Fuegner(D) MZ, E. Degner(D) MZ.

500 cc: 1 J. Surtees(GB) MV 84.85 mph, 2 B. Brown(AUS) Norton, 3 R. Venturi(I) MV, 4 D. Dale(GB) BMW, 5 J. Redman(Rhod) Norton, 6 R. Miles(AUS) Norton.

Sidecar: 1 F. Camathias(CH)/H. Cecco(D) BMW 74.51 mph, 2 P. Harris/R. Campbell(GB) Norton, 3 H. Fath/A. Wohlgemuth(D) BMW, 4 E. Strub/J. Siffert(CH) BMW, 5 B. Boddice/B. Canning(GB) Norton, 6 L. Neussner(D)/T. Partige(GB) BMW.

Belgian GP (Spa)

125 cc: 1 C. Ubbiali(I) MV 98.76 mph, 2 T. Provini(I) MV, 3 L. Taveri(CH) Ducati, 4 D. Minter(GB) MZ, 5 K. Kavanagh(AUS) Ducati, 6 K. Kronmuller(D) Ducati.

500 cc: 1 J. Surtees(GB) MV 119.20 mph, 2 G. Hocking (Rhod) Norton, 3 G. Duke(GB) Norton, 4 B. Brown(AUS) Norton, 5 R. Venturi(I) MV, 6 B. Anderson(GB) Norton.

Sidecar: 1 W. Schneider/H. Strauss(D) BMW 99.72 mph, 2 J. Rogliardo/M. Godillot(F) BMW, 3 F. Scheidegger (CH)/H. Burckhardt(D) BMW, 4 E. Strub/J. Siffert(CH) BMW, 5 B. Beevers/J. Chisnell(GB) BMW, 6 J. Duhem/R. Burtin(F) BMW.

Swedish GP (Kristianstad)

125 cc: 1 T. Provini(I) MV 82.44 mph, 2 C. Ubbiali(I) MV, 3 W. Musiol(D) MZ, 4 M. Hailwood(GB) Ducati, 5 K. Kavanagh(AUS) Ducati, 6 O. Svensson(SW) Ducati.

250 cc: 1 G. Hocking(Rhod) MZ 86.94 mph, 2 C. Ubbiali (I) MV, 3 G. Duke(GB) Benelli, 4 E. Degner(D) MZ, 5 M. Hailwood(GB) Mondial, 6 D. Dale(GB) Benelli.

350 cc: 1 J. Surtees(GB) 93.08 mph, 2 J. Hartle(GB) MV, 3 B. Brown(AUS) Norton, 4 D. Dale(GB) AJS, 5 M. Hailwood(GB) AJS, 6 J. Redman(Rhod) Norton.

Ulster GP

125 cc: 1 M. Hailwood(GB) Ducati 81.90 mph, 2 G. Hocking(Rhod) MZ, 3 E. Degner(D) MZ, 4 K. Kavanagh(AUS) Ducati, 5 A. Pagani(I) Ducati, 6 A. Wheeter(GB) Ducati.

250 cc: 1 G. Hocking(Rhod) MZ 89.37 mph, 2 M. Hailwood(GB) Mondial, 3 E. Degner(D) MZ, 4 T. Robb(GB) BMS, 5 P. Carter(GB) NSU, 6 G. Beer(D) Adler.

350 cc: 1 J. Surtees(GB) MV 91.24 mph, 2 B. Brown(AUS) Norton, 3 G. Duke(GB) Gilera, 4 D. Dale(GB) AJS, 5 T. Phillis(AUS) Norton, 6 J. Hempleman(NZ) Norton.

500 cc: 1 J. Surtees(GB) MV 95.20 mph, 2 B. McIntyre (GB) Norton, 3 G. Duke(GB) Norton, 4 T. Shepherd(GB) Norton, 5 B. Brown(AUS), 6 A. King(GB) Norton.

Italian GP (Monza)

125 cc: 1 E. Degner(D) MZ 96.08 mph, 2 C. Ubbiali(I) MV, 3 L. Taveri(CH) Ducati, 4 D. Minter(GB) MZ, 5 T. Provini(I) MV, 6 G. Hocking(Rhod) MV.

250 cc: 1 C. Ubbiali(I) MV 107.46 mph, 2 E. Degner(D) MZ, 3 E. Mendogni(I) Morini, 4 D. Minter(GB) Morini, 5 L. Taveri(CH) MZ, 6 T. Robb(GB) MZ.

350 cc: 1 J. Surtees(GB) MV 107.08 mph, 2 R. Venturi(I) MV, 3 B. Brown(AUS) Norton, 4 J. Hempleman(NZ) Norton, 5 P. Driver(SA) Norton, 6 G. Milani(I) Norton.

500 cc 1 J. Surtees(GB) MV 115.15 mph, 2 R. Venturi(I) MV, 3 G. Duke(GB) Norton, 4 B. Brown(AUS) Norton, 5 J. Hempleman(NZ) Norton, 6 P. Driver(SA) Norton.

World champions

125 cc: 1 C. Ubbiali(I) MV, 2 T. Provini(I) MV,
3 M. Hailwood(GB) Ducati).

250 cc: 1 C. Ubbiali(I) MV, 2 T. Provini(I) MV,
3 G. Hocking(Rhod) MZ.

350 cc: 1 J. Surtees(GB) MV, 2 J. Hartle(GB) MV,
3 B. Brown(AUS) Norton.

500 cc: 1 J. Surtees(GB) MV, 2 R. Venturi(I) MV,
3 B. Brown(AUS) Norton.

Sidecar: 1 W. Schneider(D) BMW, 2 F. Camathias(CH)
BMW, 3 F. Scheidegger(CH) BMW.

Acknowledgements

In researching a period of sporting history which had run its course before I was out of short trousers I have quite naturally been heavily dependent upon information from many experts from that era.

Without them I would not have been able to bring together these facts and figures under one cover. They include journalists, authors, riders, mechanics and enthusiasts—all too numerous to list. But there are exceptions without mention of whom this volume would be incomplete.

I would like to extend my thanks in particular to Vic Willoughby, former rider and technical editor with *Motor Cycle* (now *Motor Cycle Weekly*) who cast his eye over my work to ensure authenticity and accuracy. Also to his fellow authors, Richard Renstrom, Roy Bacon, Jeff Clew, Dennis May, C. S. Davidson, Phil Heath, John Griffith, Norman Windrum, Roland Bettex and Gaston Corthesy.

I would also like to thank the trade press and in particular *Motor Cycle Weekly*, *Motor Cycle News*, *Classic Bike* magazine and the *Motor Cycling Year Books* from 1950–59.

And then there are my good friends the photographers who scoured their files to come up with the truly amazing array of illustrations. Nick Nicholls, Don Morley and Tom March were an invaluable source of photographic evidence and a host of other contributors included the Associated Press, Cyril Ayton, editor of *Motorcycle Sport*, James Cowe, Micro Decet, Phil Heath, Bob Holliday, J. W. Kitchenham, Wilson McComb, the National Motor Museum, Publifoto Milan, Mick Woollett, editor of *Motor Cycle Weekly*, and Italian archivist Franco Zagari.

Finally I would like to thank the riders, designers and engineers of the 1950s for providing me with such a fascinating period of history to write about.

AMcK